"What a terrific read! C-4 is chock-full of insights on how to ignite your career. Winton nails it!"

—**Rob Carter**,
Executive Vice President & Chief Information Officer, FedEx Corporation

"Chris Winton is a masterful storyteller who knows how to capture the readers' attention with sensational real life experiences and an amazing framework that can assist and propel you in your life. This is a must read if you want to continue to charter the course for your career and grow as a leader, mom, dad, brother, sister, or individual. The stories are so vivid, which allows you to continue to reflect on your own personal journey. A must read!"

—**Cisco Sanchez**,
IT Senior Vice-President & Chief Information Officer, FedEx Ground

"I've read a plethora of personal growth books over the years. However, the practical insights, learnings and wisdom that Chris Winton expounds in this book is game changing. I call it "Winsdom" (Winton Wisdom)."

—**Thanh Anderson**,
Vice-President, Human Resources, FedEx Logistics

"I watched Chris transform mindsets as we worked together on the local workforce board. He is fully committed to connecting people with possibilities in the Memphis community. This C-4 Approach provides a framework that is scalable to any community."

—**KEVIN WOODS,**
Memphis Market President, BlueCross BlueShield of Tennessee & Shelby County Schools Board Member

"Chris ignites excitement and creates opportunities of hope in people where they can realize their potential. He did it for me and I'm excited to see him put it into a book for others to use."

—**DR. MARIO BROWN,**
Chief Talent Development Officer, First Horizon Bank

"The 4 Cs individually are simple words used as part of the everyday leadership vernacular landscape. However, C-4 strategically threaded through everyday interactions with your team is powerful and impactful. Through purposeful application of the C-4 Approach, I have watched my team go from an effective group of team members, to a highly successful and admired team of professionals leading their peers and business partner to the highest levels of interconnectedness and achievement. I have also used the C-4 framework in my personal life where I find that my family listens and communicates better, is more connected and closer than ever before. I am a true believer of this wonderful method!"

—**ALYSSA MOLINA,**
Director, Human Resources

Chris has an electric energy that is contagious and ignites focus and movement. His C-4 methodology transcends beyond professional platforms and can easily influence personal experiences.

—**TRACEE WALLS,**
Diversity & Inclusion Manager

"In *C-4 Leadership*, Chris challenges our fortitude, discretion and hearts in ways we don't naturally succumb to as leaders. He inspires, exhorts and dares us to find our measured calling of service, accountability and personal growth. This book is a strong witness to the amazing and improbable outcomes that occur when we tie our beliefs and experiences to our highest ideals – we can reach for and attain the seemingly impossible. Winton is real, engaging, and impactful. His C-4 Approach is explosive in the best of ways!"

—**TONY SHARP**

"The C-4 Approach lets Chris Winton transfer his unique success to others. Buckle your seatbelt, because you are in for one of the greatest rides of your life!"

ANTHONY M. FLYNN
Founder & CEO of AmazingCEO.com

C-4

LEADERSHIP

IGNITE YOUR CAREER
SHATTER EXPECTATIONS
TAKE CHARGE OF YOUR LIFE

CHRIS WINTON

PRESS

I dedicate this book to the three people who keep me lifted everyday, my wife Coleshia and my two kids, Jordyn and Jaden.

CONTENTS

CHAPTER 1

YOUR GLASS CEILING

HOW THE HELL *did you do that?*

That's the question I'm most often asked when people hear my story.

My story probably started out pretty normal. I grew up as an African-American kid in inner-city Memphis. Although I aced elementary school, I was a C-student in high school because I was juggling two jobs to help make ends meet.

When I got my first Information Systems (IT) job after college, I had a chip on my shoulder that was so big, I'm surprised it—and my head—fit through the door. Worse, I thought I *deserved* a leadership position.

When my first boss asked me what I wanted to accomplish I told him I wanted *his job*. I wanted to be the boss and tell people what to do.

If my attitude—and my thinking about leadership—hadn't changed, I would never have gotten to where I am today.

Fast forward to today: I became a Vice President of Human Resources at FedEx at age 39. I'm routinely asked to speak to tech companies like Google and *The White House* about hiring processes and leadership development. But I truly realized how far I'd come, and how much I had changed when I was first invited to sit at the table with FedEx founder and Chairman, Fred Smith.

When he first walked into the room, my heart started pounding. He sat down and shuffled some papers, before looking off in the distance as if thinking deeply about something. I shifted awkwardly, hoping no one could sense how much I felt like an imposter in that moment.

Then Fred stood, walked around the table to me, and stuck out his hand: "Hi, I'm Fred Smith." I grasped his hand and replied, "Chris Winton, VP of Human Resources."

He smiled and said the words I'll never forget: "I know. Welcome Chris, I'm glad you're here."

In that moment, I realized I had come a long way—from C-student to C-suite.

How the hell *did* I do that? I'm glad you asked.

THE QBQ

One thing I've learned on the journey is that often the question we *do* ask isn't the question we *really* want to ask. John G. Miller wrote about this reality in his book *QBQ! The Question Behind the Question.* As he noted, we may test the waters with the first question, before asking what we really want to ask.

So, if I may be so bold, when people ask me *How the hell did you do that?* What they really want to know, the QBQ, is this: *How can I do that?*

If you're wondering the same thing, stick around. Maybe you picked up this book because you're just getting started as a leader and want to ignite your career success (instead of watching it go up in flames). Maybe you're already leading in middle management, but you've got your sights set on the C-suite. And you're wondering how to crack the promotion code.

Perhaps you're great at what you do in the corporate space, but—for reasons you can't quite explain—you've stalled where you are. Or maybe you're like me and you've spent your entire career on a certain track, but lately you've been thinking of making a change.

It doesn't matter where you are positionally, most people in the corporate business world want similar things: move up the corporate ladder, be entrusted with greater responsibility, expand influence and prestige, make more money—and still enjoy life.

But a lot of people struggle to climb that corporate success ladder. It's not an easy climb and, even if you can see it, it can look blocked for you.

I get it. I've been there.

I've stood at the bottom and looked up with that same mix of confusion, envy, and frustration. I understand what it's like to feel:

> ➤ **STUCK** —You know where you want to go, but you can't see how to get there. You feel mired down in your day-to-day crises and tedious tasks. You can't make any progress toward your career goals.

> ➤ **OVERLOOKED** —You want to get noticed, but you feel invisible. You may have started bright-eyed and head-up, but now you feel ignored and beaten down. You feel like nothing you do really matters, so why do anything more than the minimum?

> ➤ **UNAPPRECIATED** —You started out ready to take on the world and tackle any project, no matter how big, but your efforts yielded little praise or financial reward. So now you figure, Why bother?

> ➤ **DISCRIMINATED AGAINST** —Maybe, like me, you're a minority or someone who doesn't quite look or act like everyone else. There's a network that you aren't part of so you feel like you're on the outside looking in, and the deck is stacked against you.

➤ **ENTITLED** —Maybe you have a big chip on your shoulder and you're just daring someone to knock it off. You know you're better than "they" are and don't understand why your bosses can't see it, too.

With all of these feelings, and many others, the question behind the question is this: How can you break through the glass ceiling to achieve the success you've always dreamed of?

You may think you are being held back because of *who* you are. But are you really? For example, maybe you think it's because you...

➤ **COME FROM THE WRONG NEIGHBORHOOD.** (I'm from inner-city Memphis, remember. With that logic, I shouldn't be here.)

➤ **DIDN'T MAKE STRAIGHT AS.** (Me neither. Join the club.)

➤ **HATED TO READ.** (I didn't read my first book until I was 26—yes, you read that right.)

➤ **WEREN'T BORN TO PRIVILEGE.** (I'm the son of two amazing blue-collar parents who often worked two or even three jobs.)

➤ **[FILL IN YOUR OWN UNIQUE EXCUSES HERE.]**

But do those factors really create a glass ceiling for you? Here's a counterintuitive thought: what if your glass ceiling *isn't really made of glass?* In fact, what if it's merely something *you've* created that can be easily shattered with the right tools and know-how?

Hmmm. Maybe it's time to look differently at what's holding you back.

On my journey to success, I've learned that none of these things *have* to hold you back. In fact, from my experience coaching people from diverse backgrounds, the "glass ceiling" concept isn't limited to people of color, women, or people with differences. People in every demographic group complain equally about it. It's an equal-opportunity *dis*-abler.

Everyone seems tempted to think that there is a unique glass ceiling designed to keep him or her down. But I've found that there's also a commonality amongst those who've broken through and now lead from the other side.

HE AIN'T HEAVY

When I was in high school I worked two jobs. That was why I was a C-student. I didn't have time to study. In my senior year, I had a work permit to leave school early each day. But one day, a guidance counselor stopped me in the hallway and invited me to attend a presentation from an organization called INROADS.

This group focused on identifying top minority talent (I guess they hadn't seen my grades) and giving that talent an early start in corporate leadership training. I agreed to go and hear more of what it was about, but it didn't take long to hear a problem: I needed a 3.0 minimum GPA.

I knew I didn't have that, so I got up to walk out. My counselor stopped me just outside the door and told me they wanted to talk to me anyway. Apparently, she had told them I was already a supervisor at my job. The fact that I was already in a leadership role while in high school intrigued them enough to take a chance on me.

So, a few days later I went to the Memphis chapter of INROADS and met a man named Alfonzo Alexander. He was built like a linebacker in football with the voice of Morpheus in the Matrix. This man would become my very first mentor and, ultimately, a dear friend.

One day, he called me into his office to get some background info on me. His first question: "So what *do* you want to be ten years from now?"

With all the teenage arrogance I could muster, I said, "I want to be the CEO of a Fortune 500 company." (Truth be told, I wasn't exactly sure what that was.)

Alfonzo looked at me across his desk and simply said, "CEO, huh?"

With unwavering confidence, I spelled it out for him, "C-E-O."

He stared at me for a minute, tapping his fingers on the well-worn desk. Finally, he said, "I tell you what," he turned toward a picture hanging on the wall, "Look at this picture and tell me what you see." I looked and saw what I would later learn was a picture by the artist Gilbert Young titled *He Ain't Heavy.* In it, a muscular black man is leaning over a wall, straining to reach another person below the canvas whose hand reaches up. I couldn't see either face, but my eye was drawn to the effort both people seemed to be making to reach each other.

After giving the picture a quick look, I told Alfonzo it looked like someone needs help, and the other person is reaching down to help him. He calmly shook his head. "You missed it." Well, I knew I was only a C-student, but clearly there was one hand reaching down and one reaching up. Someone needed help, and someone else was helping. So I tried again, trying to make it sound like I understood.

"I get it. If you want to be a leader, you've got to be willing to reach down and pull people up."

"Nope, You still missed it." At that point I had nothing. So I simply shrugged.

Alfonzo turned back to look me in the eye and explained, "If you ever want to be a leader, you should be *both* hands at all times. The posture of leadership is this: One hand always reaching up. One hand always reaching down."

That day with Alfonzo started to change my thinking about what it means to be a leader and *why* I wanted to lead. I had never really thought about reaching others at all. I figured I'd need both hands to claw my way to the top.

It wasn't always smooth sailing from there, but whenever I hit the rough patches, that image would always come to mind. In fact, I now have that same painting hanging in my office. I often turn to it when someone tells me they want to be a leader.

That day taught me that leadership is more about posture than position. It's about being authentic and vulnerable. After all, if you have one hand reaching up and one hand reaching down, you're in a vulnerable position. Your heart, the core of who you are, gets exposed. It's a scary and potentially painful place to be. But it's where you realize the highest and best rewards.

THE BUMPY ROAD TO THE TOP

In the four years I was with Alfonzo at INROADS, I learned to dress, talk, and act like a professional leader. I stopped thinking of myself as an inner-city Memphis kid who made Cs and barely got through school and started thinking of myself as a professional.

One of the things Alfonzo encouraged me to do was to write in a journal every day. He told me to cast a vision for ten years in the future. So I did. I had a vision for my future and was developing the confidence to achieve it.

What could go wrong? I'd be a C-E-O in no time. To be candid, I'm glad it didn't quite work that way. Otherwise I wouldn't have all the stories to share with you in this book.

I spent the next four summers with INROADS, training all day on Saturday in a suit and tie and working through internships Monday through Friday. I learned that I had a gift for computers and was good at Information Technology, so I enrolled in the University of Memphis in the newly formed Management Information Systems program.

After getting my degree, I got a job at FedEx working in the IT department as a Computer Technician. I already told you I was cocky and self-assured, but I was also good at my job and I rose through the ranks. When the opportunity to move to Atlanta and work as a field consultant came up, I jumped at the chance. It seemed like a good career move. But when I started unpacking boxes in my new house, there at the bottom was my worn journal from INROADS. One look at the words on the page caused me to start wondering if I'd made a big mistake.

This was a season where I was moving up in my career. I was working hard, newly married, and had a happy home life. I bought the house, had nice cars in the garage, and appeared to be the picture of success from the outside. I'd gone from unsure intern, to cocky amateur, to a gifted professional.

Yet one day, I ended up sitting in my car, hands on the wheel as I stared ahead, feeling frustrated and thinking, *What in the world am I doing here?* I seemed to have it all yet, deep down, I wasn't feeling fulfilled.

I was climbing the ladder, but was beginning to wonder, *What if my ladder is leaning against the wrong wall?*

One look at my journal and I realized that I wasn't even close to the goal I had set for myself. In fact, I was drifting. Was I successful? Yes. But what's the point of being successful if it leaves you feeling empty? Something needed to change, and it would take courage to make it happen. I enrolled in an MBA program thinking this was the next logical next.

The one thing that never changed was my desire to help the people I worked with. I always worked to improve my leadership style even as I rose through the ranks at FedEx. It wasn't easy, but the new climb was worth it.

How did I do it?

I learned a process that made all the difference and earned me a seat at the C-suite table.

It's called *C-4 Leadership.*

WHAT IS C-4 LEADERSHIP?

In my twenty years at FedEx, I noticed a pattern other leaders followed that I call C-4 Leadership. As it transformed my thinking, I started to change the way I led myself. As a result, I changed and positioned myself to lead as I made these four steps part of my climb to the top:

➤ **CONSUME:** You must be a consumer of information, but what you consume is important. Learning to consume the right information, at the right time, is critical to leadership growth.

➤ **CONNECT:** Information is useless until you learn to connect the dots. This helps you use your insights to reach your goals and objectives in the fastest way possible while helping others do the same. Then others will begin to know what you know.

➤ **COMMUNICATE:** The best leaders have an uncanny ability to stand up and articulate a clear message and get people galvanized around a common idea. They turn ideas into action.

➤ **COACH:** Leaders must reach up and down. Coaching others helps them connect their personal goals to the business goals so that both the person and the professional reach new heights.

The glass ceiling can be incredibly strong—until you hit it just right. Hit it with the right explosive transfer of energy and what happens? It shatters.

You need an explosion to crash through *your* glass ceiling, whatever that is for you. Leadership growth is like an explosion. But you don't need to be a demolitions expert to realize that explosions can be dangerous if they aren't controlled.

Blow up at the wrong time or in the wrong way, and you destroy everything around you. Blow up in the right way, however, and you rapidly remove obstacles to reach your objectives.

C-4 Leadership is all about exploding in the right way, at the right time, and in the right direction. Leaders must be moldable, flexible, stable, and not easily detonated.

Right now you may think you're staring at a career ceiling made of unbreakable glass. But in the pages that follow, I'll show you how to shatter it and ignite your career success. The explosive C-4 is powerful—when handled with care. C-4 Leadership is also powerful—when you use it in the right way. So let's start putting it to work for you.

CHAPTER 2

WHY C-4?

C-4. YOU'VE HEARD of it. You've probably seen an action-movie hero use a pinkish block of clay-like substance to blow open a safe, knock down a door, or take out "the bad guys."

An early form of C-4 was first invented by the British during World War II, and later introduced to the American military as Compound C. Versions C2 and C3 were violent, but unstable, so the chemical compositions were changed. What we now know as C-4 was introduced in the 1950s.

The idea behind C-4 is simple. Mix explosive chemicals with a plastic binder material and you've got something incredibly stable *until* just the right amount of heat and pressure make it go *boom!*

Think Silly Putty, but with attitude.

C-4 was a major step forward from dynamite, which itself was a step up from nitroglycerin. Liquid nitroglycerin was extremely volatile. (Just like some leaders I've known.) Bump a vial of liquid nitroglycerin, and it could explode. Dynamite was more stable than that. It was made of a core of absorbent material like sawdust, then soaked in liquid nitroglycerin.

Add a blasting cap, and you've got a powerful explosion.

But a stick of dynamite still risks all kinds of collateral damage. It's not moldable. It's only moderately stable, and it doesn't respond well to heat, pressure, and stress.

On the other hand, C-4 provides a powerful burst of energy that destroys obstacles and provides a clear path forward. C-4 can be pressed into gaps, cracks, voids, and molded into any shape to achieve the desired objective. It's stable and resists most physical shocks. It can't be detonated by gunshot, dropping on a hard surface, being set on fire, or microwave radiation.

It can *only* be detonated by a combination of extreme *heat* and *pressure*.

Since C-4 was created to be stable, it takes a considerable amount of effort to set it off. You can light it with a match. It will slowly burn, but not explode. You can shoot it with a rifle, but it won't do anything. Add a detonator in a controlled fashion, however, and you create the extreme heat and pressure needed to activate the compound and cause a fantastic explosion.

Do you see the leadership connection? Lighting a stick of dynamite and tossing it into a mineshaft might look cool on television, but it probably won't help you find any gold. Instead, you'll be choking on a smoky cloud of dust that blocks your view and keeps you from making progress.

Yet that's how many frustrated people tackle career obstacles. They make a lot of noise and spend a ton of energy, but have little to show for it. They're still trapped under a glass ceiling of their own making. And when they blast off, the collateral damage shoots in all directions. I call this *dynamite leadership*. And I don't mean it in a good way.

Only when you control the blast by strategically shaping the charge can you remove the rock and get the treasure beneath. C-4 plastic explosives provide an easily molded, malleable, stable, and controlled explosion that does what it's supposed to do, when and where it's supposed to do it. C-4 Leadership works in much the same way.

DYNAMITE LEADERSHIP VS. C-4 LEADERSHIP

Maybe you've felt the repercussions of dynamite leadership. You've worked for a leader whose idea of leading was lighting the fuse, tossing a stick of dynamite into the middle of the team, ducking around the corner with eyes clamped shut and hands covering ears. Then they show up after the dust settles to see if the obstacle has been removed.

The irony is that leaders like this—dynamite leaders—think this action is a good thing. In fact, *dynamite leader* even sounds positive, but the effects can be devastating. They mistakenly believe that this method of leading forces their team to adapt to adversity and rise to the challenge under pressure. They go around starting fires, leaving their people to clean up the mess.

But it doesn't take a genius to see why this approach is foolish. People may survive one explosion. Or two. Maybe even three. But before long, if you're a dynamite leader, they will flinch whenever you walk into a room. They can't trust you because they never know when or what you might detonate. And with unfocused detonation comes high collateral damage. Nobody wants to be your collateral damage.

Like explosives, perceptions of leadership have changed. The best leaders aren't authoritarian dictators who blow up if things aren't done their way. They don't use dynamite to blast through their glass ceiling, because they know the chaos that can ensue. The best leaders know how to adjust to changing conditions.

Bottom line: dynamite leadership can be incredibly destructive to organizations and the people in them, with the impact extending to their families and communities.

But C-4 Leadership is an entirely different story. There are a few critical differences between C-4 Leadership and Dynamite Leadership:

➤ **C-4 LEADERSHIP IS INTENTIONAL. Dynamite Leadership is** *light the fuse and run.* Everything about C-4 Leadership is intentional. It's done with care. From how and where it is applied, how much is needed, and when to detonate—the C-4 Leader leaves nothing to chance.

➤ **C-4 LEADERSHIP IS FOCUSED. Dynamite Leadership is** *toss it in and cover your ears.* C-4 Leadership is highly focused. To bring down a building, demolition experts know exactly where to place the charges to yield the maximum impact. C-4 Leaders work in the same way. They assess the situation and focus their impact where and when it is needed. Dynamite Leaders make a big explosion, but do little actual good and quite a bit of harm.

➤ **C-4 LEADERSHIP IS SHAPED. Dynamite Leadership is** *a one-size-fits-all approach.* C-4 Leaders know that because people are different, the way they should be led is different. They shape their leadership in a way that does the most good for the situation at hand. It's flexible and works with the situation. Dynamite Leadership is rigid and unyielding.

➤ **C-4 LEADERSHIP IS STABLE. Dynamite Leadership is** *volatile—don't bump this or BOOM!* C-4 Leadership, like C-4, is stable. It isn't easily detonated and weathers the shocks of life. C-4 Leaders provide a stable presence for their team. They can be counted on no matter how turbulent things are around them. Dynamite Leadership is volatile. It's as unstable as the nitroglycerin in a stick of dynamite. *One wrong move and BOOM!*

THE VALUE OF C-4

Explosions on their own are neither good nor bad. What makes them good or bad is when and where they happen. C-4 packed around the structural supports of a run-down building in the heart of the city can be good—if the aim is to make room for a new structure that brings in business and revenue. C-4 strapped to the underside of a bus with a timer rigged to blow if the bus drops below 50 MPH— well, you've probably seen the movie.

The difference is in how it's used.

C-4 is simply a tool. And C-4 Leaders use the best properties of C-4 to frame the way they lead themselves and lead others. To lead in today's rapidly shifting business environment, leaders must flex with the changes. Those who remain stuck in their way of doing things will quickly get left behind. The best leaders are moldable, shapeable, and fill in the gaps on their team.

Leaders also must have the right kind of attitude. They must be willing to do whatever it takes to help the team win. C-4 Leaders must have big hearts and a willingness to serve.

I got my first taste of this when I was nine years old. I played little league football with the Southeast Memphis Athletic Association. It's probably safe to say I was the smallest kid on our team called the Rebels. I'm five foot five now, and like I like to say I've been this height my whole life. But at nine years old, I was even shorter.

The beauty of little league football is that you need eleven players on the field. Since we typically only had twelve or thirteen kids on the roster, I got to play every game. So naturally, the coach put me in as a tight end. In the NFL, tight ends are usually 6'5" or taller, about 265 pounds of solid muscle. Plus they run fast, have an amazing vertical leap, and hands that can catch anything. Oh yeah, and they're hard to tackle. Basically, everything I *wasn't* as a kid.

Needless to say, I didn't get many passes thrown my way. But I did become the best blocker I knew how to be. I didn't stop there. I decided to spend a lot of time learning the play book. During one game, the wing back got hurt, and the coach was frustrated. He looked at the sideline and didn't have a lot of depth on the bench.

I didn't have much to lose, so I walked up to the coach and said, "Coach, I can play wing back." He glanced down at me and asked if I knew the plays. I said yes. So that week in practice I played wingback, and during the next game I was the starting wingback. Two games later, the tailback got hurt. In little league, you trip, fall, and twist an ankle, and you're out. Another one bites the dust. The Rebels were dropping like flies.

My coach had the same puzzled look on his face, so I walked up and said, "Coach, I can play tailback." He asked, "Do you know the plays from the tailback position?" I said, "Yeah. I've been looking at the playbook all season. I can play tailback." Over the next couple games, I lined up at tailback and got to carry the ball.

But the string of bad luck and injuries didn't stop there. The quarterback was the next player to get hurt. Now the coach didn't even hesitate. He looked over at me and said, "Is there any chance you've paid attention to the plays from the quarterback position?" I said, "Actually, yes. I can play quarterback." I played the quarterback position for the rest of the season.

Now, I would like to say that I was the fastest kid on the team. But I wasn't. I wasn't the biggest, and we didn't win at all. But I learned a great deal about leadership that season. And at the end of the year banquet, when the coach announced the Most Valuable Player award, he said:

This trophy typically goes to the kid that scores the most touchdowns. Or the kid that makes the most tackles. This year, this kid's neither. He literally was the person we needed when we needed him, and that's what made him the MVP.

When he called my name, I walked past the all banged-up members of the Southeast Memphis Athletic Association Rebels to accept the honor.

That lesson has stuck with me for years, because I still don't consider myself the smartest, the fastest, or the best. But as a leader, I've always made sure to study all of the positions wherever I am and *fill the gap*.

The lesson is simple: when you fill the gap, the team wins. It's amazing how doing that can start to propel your career. Every coach and every leader is looking for someone that is studying all positions, not just their own. Be that kind of person and you've mastered the first requirement of C-4 Leadership.

BE STABLE AND RESISTANT TO SHOCKS

Not only must C-4 Leaders be moldable and ready and willing to fill the gaps, they also must be stable and resistant to shocks. The crazy thing about life is, you don't know when and where the shock will come from. That's why it's so important to be prepared when it happens.

When I was fifteen, I got my first real job at Dan's Big Star, a local grocery store. I was a sacker, working for $3 an hour. The little old ladies that would come in *loved* for me to carry their groceries out so much that they would give a big fifty cent tip. I worked there for about eighteen months and got promoted to supervisor over customer service.

That was a lot of responsibility for a sixteen-year-old kid at the time. It included counting down the money in the safe for the night. One night we were closing the store down. It was just me and one of the on-duty managers that night. The store was empty, when suddenly someone came running in. I had my head down, counting the money so I didn't see him at first, but my peer manager did and bolted out the back door. *Uh, thanks. See you later. I guess I got this.*

By the time I looked up, there was a gun inches from my face, and a jittery, would-be robber yelling, "Give me the money!"

After that point, everything else is a blur. All I remember is dumping money out and loading it in the bag. The robber ran out the doors and left me sitting, shaken, but unharmed on the floor in front of the now-empty safe. Apparently, my manager had called the police, because they showed up soon after. They called my parents who hurried down to the store.

After I gave my report to the police, my parents took me home. Of course, I was shocked and shaken. I was only sixteen and wanted to quit. But my dad gave me some tough love that stuck with me. He said, "We don't quit. Matter of fact, you're going back to work tomorrow." He knew that if I let the shock of that experience stick with me that it would start a pattern that would be hard to break.

So, I went back to work. Things slowly returned to normal, and then, three months later, we got robbed again. But this time—since it was a small, family-owned store—we had a gun behind the counter in customer service. When the robbers came in, they jumped the counter and slid into the customer service area. The owner was there, and they landed on top of him. He was a big guy, a former wrestler, so he tackled the robber, and pinned him down. But in the tussle, the robber's gun went off.

Another manager, John Russell, was in the back. He heard the shot and ran to the front. When he saw the tussle going on, he pulled out his gun and shot the robber. Sadly, he didn't know there were two more robbers in the store. One of them came behind him, shot him in the back, and killed him.

That tragic event happened in the morning while I was at school. I was scheduled to work that night. Obviously, I was pretty upset when I heard the news because I looked up to John Russell and Robbie, the owner, who was also shot in the whole ordeal.

I went home after school and same as last time, I said, "I'm not going to work. I'm pretty sure the store is not even going to be open." But my Dad said to call up there and see. So I called, and they had only closed the store for a couple of hours. The store was going to be open that night.

I looked at my dad, and he said, "Then you go to work." Then he said, "You fall down son, you get back up. Life is going to hit you. But you've got to press through it." So that night I literally worked standing on blood-soaked carpet.

That kind of experience sticks with you. But it also gives you a core of inner strength. When the shock comes that could destabilize you, you've got to have a plan to press forward. Every day, leaders can encounter things that could be destabilizing if they don't have a way to remain stable and resistant to the shocks. If you are easily detonated or thrown off course, you'll always revert to dynamite leadership and the results will be catastrophic.

WHY C-4 MATTERS

C-4 Leadership is all about caring for people. If you don't care about people, then dynamite will work just fine. If the fallout doesn't phase you, then blow it up. Who cares about it? But your career will suffer and your glass ceiling will only get thicker as people apply more layers to protect themselves from you.

You can decide to break through at any cost, but you'll have shards of glass falling around you. And that hurts. It hurts you. It hurts your family. It hurts the people you lead. And ultimately it hurts your organization.

At every stage in my career, I've chosen to treat people fairly but unequally, listen for full understanding, and, when life strikes, choose to become better, not bitter.

How about you? No matter where you are on your leadership journey, you've got to continually ask yourself whether you are applying *Dynamite Leadership* to a situation that requires C-4 precision, flexibility, and stability.

It can be easy to default to the Dynamite approach, especially if that's what you've seen modeled. To what extent have you embraced Dynamite Leadership? Have you experienced it firsthand from a leader whose idea was light the fuse and run?

"Where are you going? What's holding you back?"

Maybe you are starting to recognize some of these traits in yourself and want to change. It could be you've tried a one-size-fits-all approach to leading others, and it hasn't worked out. Or maybe the shocks of life have left you feeling volatile and ready to go off at any time.

The good news is, it's never too late to start caring for people. You can explode and ignite your career in the right way, not flame out into disaster. And what you choose to do now can minimize the collateral damage as you break through your glass ceiling.

But before you learn to apply C-4 Leadership principles to your journey, there are two important questions to cover—*Where are you going?* and *What's holding you back?* Get clear on those answers and you can carefully plant the charges that will shatter your glass ceiling and unlock your upward potential.

CHAPTER 3

WHERE ARE YOU GOING?

"WHAT DO YOU want to eat?"

My wife and I were in the car looking for a place to pull in and have dinner. The kids were occupied so it was a rare chance to have a quiet moment to ourselves. I asked her where she'd like to go, knowing what she would say.

"It doesn't matter, anything's fine."

"How about that little Mexican place we like?"

"No, I don't really want that."

I was still driving down the road, watching each restaurant fade in my rearview mirror. It was time to gently ratchet up the pressure. "Ok, then, what *do* you want?"

She replied, "It doesn't matter, you just pick something."

Rafferty's was coming up on the right hand side of the road. It would be easy to whip in there. So I said, "How about Rafferty's?" She told me, "No, I had Rafferty's last week." So I zipped past Rafferty's and pulled into the parking lot of a Walmart. I stopped the car and put it in park.

Here's a pro tip: never do what I did next: "When you decide, that's when I'll start the car back up." I'll let you imagine what happened from there. Oh, boy.

A lot of people treat their careers like our search for a place to eat that night. They know they need to go somewhere, so they start moving. But they put little thought into where they are going and then they are surprised when they get somewhere they never meant to be. Or they rely on someone else to answer the question for them.

Have you ever followed someone in a car when it was clear they didn't know where they were going? It's frustrating to feel like you're wasting gas. I often tell leaders, leadership is like driving a car. For example, if we met and I thought we had started to establish some rapport I might say, *Hey, let's go grab dinner*. You'd probably get in the car with me.

If I turn on the main road and start heading east, you'd probably wonder where we were going. If I said, *Don't worry about it, I know this great place*. You may sit back and relax. But if I kept driving for forty minutes, you'd probably ask me if I was *sure* I knew where I was going. At some point, the rapport would start to break down. If I'm still driving after an hour, you're probably secretly dialing 911. You're ready to jump out in traffic because you think you've been kidnapped.

Leadership is a lot like asking people to get in the car with you. But everybody wants to know where we are going. Until you answer that question, frustration amplifies and comes out in complaints. *It's hot. It's cold. You didn't speak to me. This person isn't working well. We've got communication issues*. It's all these. They want to know: *where are we going?*

The Law of Attraction says that once your mind is set on something, you start to pull towards it. People are often so consumed with where they *are* that they can't think about where they *want to be*. There are people that are so bitter about where they are or what has happened to them to this point. There's no room in their mind to think about where they want to be.

No one else is going to take responsibility for deciding your destination. That's not a mentor's job. That's not your sponsor's job.

It's not your parents' job. It's no one else's job to figure out what job you want. That, my friend, is *completely up to you.*

"People are often so consumed with where they are that they can't think about where they want to be."

You have to be intentional about how you use the power of leadership. Are you just throwing sticks of dynamite around or do you have a destination or goal in mind? Do you know where you want to go? If you can't answer that question with clarity, you'll never be able to lead others well.

BRING ON THE HEAT

You'll never have a C-4 Leadership explosion unless you first have heat. One of the things that makes C-4 explosive so versatile is its stability. It will not blow up unless you add heat. But with that heat comes a small spark that detonates into a big explosion.

The clarity you need for your journey works in much the same way. Without the spark that clarity brings, you'll sit dormant, static, with no sense of direction and no urgency to get there. You might as well be driving without directions.

Sometimes the spark you need happens on its own, but it's much more effective when you seek out clarity and apply it to your life. I first felt the heat when I walked into my internship at INROADS early one Saturday morning.

I can remember feeling physically hot as I tied my tie around my neck and cinched the knot tight. Alfonzo told us we had to dress in full business attire. I didn't even own a suit, so I'd spent the previous week tracking down a navy blue suit, a white shirt, a red or a blue tie, and dark shoes. It seemed that professionalism had a very specific look. I looked at myself in the mirror and thought I was pulling it off well. But Memphis in the summer was *hot,* and I could feel myself sweating under my clothes.

When I walked into the room at the University of Memphis, there stood Alfonzo. Alfonzo played as a defensive player in college, so he commanded the room in his crisp navy blue suit, white shirt, and red power tie. From his head to his feet, he modeled the look of a powerful, black man.

He looked down at me that morning and said, "Mr. Winton, looking good today. Come on in." I puffed up my chest a little bit and stood a little taller. Every day before you showed up for a session, they checked you head to toe. If you were not dressed appropriately, you did not get to attend. And if you missed two sessions, you were out of the program.

I could sense something starting to change in me that first morning. I had come into the program feeling like I hadn't earned it, so I felt pressure to work harder than everybody else. I believed I needed to be the first one there and the last one to leave. In my mind, I was only a C-student. And even though there was a good reason for that, I was sensitive to the fact that I wasn't smarter than everyone else. If I couldn't outsmart them, I decided to outwork them.

As Alfonzo looked at the dozen or so young men and women staring back at us, he issued our first challenge: *remember the mission.* He then explained what that meant and began to drill it into our heads. The next week, when we came in, he asked, "What's the mission of INROADS?" My hand shot up like a rocket. "The mission of INROADS is to develop and place talented minority youth in business and industry, and prepare them for corporate and community leadership."

After twenty-four years, I can still remember it like it was yesterday. That part of my life ended a long time ago, but it set the foundation of discipline and the practice of being intentional. It was the spark I needed to bring clarity to my life. It's fair to say that it was the explosion that launched me on my leadership journey.

Before that day, I was a hard worker, but I was directionless. I was moving for the sake of movement. After that day, and for the next four years with INROADS, I built the foundation for the leader I would become.

That first day, Alfonzo challenged me to buy a journal. He said, "Write down ten years from now what you want to be doing." That is the roadmap that will bring you clarity. He was right. What started that day changed the direction of my life.

I decided to set my sights a little lower than CEO and shoot for something I could reasonably attain in the next ten years. It would still be a challenge, but it was a doable challenge. Alfonzo walked me backwards from where I wanted to be to where I was at that moment. I knew I wanted to be in some kind of leadership, so I set a goal to become an Information Systems Manager within the next ten years. I felt a little silly, but I wrote it down in my journal.

Over the next four years, trusty journal at my side, I transformed from a hard-working but directionless kid, to a hard-working and focused college student. As new goals came to mind, I added them to my journal. I started my career at FedEx and got off track a few times, but that journal always provided the spark and clarity to refocus and move forward.

Eight months shy of my ten year goal, I looked at the sign on my door. It read: *Chris Winton, Information Systems Manager.* It was time for a new goal.

FROM C-STUDENT TO C-SUITE

We all get somewhere in life. A few people get somewhere on purpose. They think critically about where they want to go. They strike out on their own path. They know where they want to succeed and formulate a plan to make it happen. They pivot when necessary—and trust me, it's often necessary. They are prepared for opportunity.

You'll never shatter your glass ceiling unless you find your own path.

When you are a kid, if you have a happy home life, you never really know what's going on behind the scenes. That was me. I grew up with two hard-working, blue-collar parents. It was a loving home and, as far as I could tell, everything was great.

"You'll never shatter your glass ceiling unless you find your own path."

As a kid, you don't know you're broke until certain things start to shift. About age eight or nine, I noticed the shift. There weren't many Christmas gifts under the tree. We were eating hotdogs and pork and beans every night. My dad picked up a second job and then a third job. My mom started working more hours as a waitress at night. We weren't poor, but we were broke.

Looking back now, I can understand how it happened. They were young, and it was tough getting jobs. My grandmother was a maid. That was the only job she could get. The only job my mom was able to obtain early on to help out her family was waitressing. In fact, she had been a waitress up until her 20s when I was born.

My dad was a janitor. He started at St. Jude. They didn't make much money, and things got even tighter when Uncle Sam showed up. My mom didn't know she had to claim tips as a waitress on her taxes, and the IRS said she owed $9,000 in back taxes. To a family of five, where dad is a janitor and mom is a waitress, a $9,000 tax bill might as well have been *nine million dollars*. It became really difficult.

They heard about this company in the city that was hiring part-time but with full-time benefits. Plus, the work was at night so they could continue their day jobs. It would add income and get us out of the hole. I remember hearing them saying *if we could just get on at FedEx everything would be better.*

One day, Mom got a call. She could start immediately at the Hub.

Dad got his call not long after and they both worked their day jobs, then came home, ate dinner, and went to work their night shift at FedEx.

This made a powerful impression on me. All my life, I'd been told to go to school, and make good grades so you don't have to work as hard. Then go to college, get your degree, get a good job with benefits so you can buy a house, finance a car, and watch the kids and dog run around inside the white picket fence. That's the American dream. It was repeated to me over and over, both at home and at school.

By the time I got to high school, I was almost on autopilot. My path had been mapped for me and I thought I was on track. I'd been a straight-A student in elementary school, but that was about to change. One night, my older brother and I were talking. We were tired of seeing our mom work so hard. We wanted to help. I started cutting grass around the neighborhood, and he got a job at McDonalds.

I soon figured out that if I cut grass and made some money, I could go to the store, stock up on candy, and sell it at school. It was brilliant. My ninth and tenth grade year became all about how I could make money to help out at home. Soon, my brother and I came up with an agreement: *We don't ask mom and dad for anything we need. We cover it ourselves.*

On one hand, I was doing great. I was working as many jobs as I could and making good money for a teenager. It was fun having money in my pocket. But something had to give and my grades were falling fast. The *A*s that I was so proud of in elementary school became *B*s, and then fell to *C*s.

I had charted my own path, and while it was successful then, I knew deep down that it wouldn't lead to the success I had in mind in the long term.

As all leaders must, I needed to decide where I wanted to succeed.

I knew that if I wanted to be more than just the entrepreneur who sold candy bars to his classmates in high school, I had to decide *where* I wanted to succeed. I had already proven that I was willing to work hard; that's how I was able to get an internship through INROADS in spite of my C-level grades. But hard work without direction wastes a lot of energy.

. . . .

"Many people fail because they have not decided where they want to succeed."

. . . .

Alfonzo had challenged me to write down my goals in the journal. But in college, a man named Professor Podgorski helped me set my career GPS. One day, after my Introduction to Business class finished, I scheduled some time during office hours to speak with the professor. We discussed the ten-year goal I had written in my journal and how I might start taking steps to get there. We began talking about combining leadership with technology. He told me about the new program at the college called Management Information Systems.

As I wrote it down in my journal, he said the words that stuck with me and changed my direction: "It's good you're writing that down because a career is like a GPS. The journey doesn't start until you set the destination."

I've replayed that analogy back in my mind over the years. He was right. The journey *doesn't* start until you actually type in the destination. A GPS can recognize where you are at this point, and plot a path. Even if you make a wrong turn, it'll plot a new path. But it can only plot the path *after* you've entered the destination.

Deciding *where* you want to succeed starts with a goal. What's your goal? Your answer to that question is foundational and sets up the entire C-4 Leadership process. Many people fail because they have not decided *where* they want to succeed. I encounter people all the time who are frustrated because they feel stuck. When I ask them where they want to go, they can't answer me. My next question: "Then how do you know you're not already there?"

Most people will tell you what they *don't* want. You can tell me you need to find another job, but until you describe the job you *do* want, I can't help you. Until you decide where you want to be, I can guarantee you one thing, you're going to stay right where you are. The journey doesn't start until you set the destination.

As I've replayed Professor Podgorski's words over and over in my head for the last twenty years, they've helped me move from position to position and from C-level student to C-suite leader. Through INROADS, I started as an IT Intern at FedEx. After I graduated, I started as an Associate Level Technician at the FedEx Memphis Hub, then was promoted to Technician. After about four years, I transferred to Atlanta as the Lead Technician and Information Systems consultant at FedEx.

With a leadership position as my ultimate goal, I applied for a manager's job *five times*. Each time I didn't get the job I kept thinking about my career GPS recalculating. It was frustrating. I knew I was still going in the right direction even if it was slower than I would have liked. I finally got my first manager's job managing a warehouse. After that, I became manager of our electronic repair team. I did that for about a year, then was Manager of Tech Support for about a year, and then at age thirty-two became Director of the Help Desk. Finally, I became the Director of IT Operations. But my journey still wasn't through.

PIVOT WHEN NECESSARY

It takes heat to bring clarity. And sometimes that heat is painful. After working as the Director of IT Operations for three and a half years, I was beat. I wasn't sleeping. I felt like it was time for a career change.

I was tired of for-profit work and, candidly, wanted to leave FedEx. My problem wasn't with the company. I felt like I wanted more meaning in the work. I wanted to make a difference. Of course, my wife thought I was crazy because, as a director, the income was pretty nice.

She knew I was tired, but figured it was just the emotional side of the job taking its toll on me. She encouraged me to push through it, but promised to listen to my plan to pivot to a new career within two years. So I put together a budget for the next two years. I figured out how to create some passive income streams. I pulled out my well-worn copy of *Rich Dad, Poor Dad* and reviewed my assets and liabilities. I started buying investment property to create a passive income stream that could replace my current income. I set a date for when I would leave FedEx.

When I got about halfway towards the goal, I happened to bump into our Director of Compensation in the cafeteria. As we talked for a bit, he said, "I was telling somebody the other day about you. Somewhere in your life, you zigged when you were supposed to zag. You got into IT, but you're really an HR guy."

I just brushed it off and laughed. I'd been in computers forever. But then, I bumped into an employee that used to work for me in the hallway. After we chatted for a minute, he said, "I was thinking about you the other night. You know you're supposed to be up on the third floor of this building, right?"

The third floor is HR. I may have been a C-student in high school, but I'm a pretty smart guy now. I had been praying that morning about leaving the company, and within five minutes, I got two messages from two different people that I should be in HR. Sometimes the heat that brings pain can also bring clarity in a blinding flash.

That week, the Director of Workforce Strategy and HR left the company. I couldn't stop thinking about what my two coworkers had said about me and HR. Could I really pivot to a whole different department? One that focused on people, not machines? I set up a meeting to talk to the Vice President of Human Resources at the time.

What she said floored me: "My biggest challenge is IT. There's this whole STEM shortage of talent, and I can't even spell IT. Having someone who could *bridge the gap* between IT and HR could be very beneficial. You should apply."

Later that evening, when I told my wife about the conversation, she just smiled. I interviewed, got the job and left IT for HR as the Director of Workforce Strategy. My first week in HR, an IT outage hit, so my previous IT operations team was in full swing. Emails were flying, bridge call was hot and heavy, and I was sitting in my new HR seat cleaning up email. Because I was still receiving all of the outage updates, I decided I should remove myself from the distribution list. I simply replied to the outage administrator, asking to "*Unsubscribe* me, please."

What I didn't realize was that I accidentally hit Reply All. *Whoops.* And, to make things worse, my unsubscribe note in the middle of the crisis went to just about every executive in the company, including the Chief Information Officer (CIO). To this day, he jokingly refers to me as *Mr. Unsubscribe.*

....

"Sometimes you do have to unsubscribe from your past to grab hold of the future."

....

Eight months later, the HR VP who brought me over decided to leave. I interviewed and became the Vice President of Human Resources. The pivot was complete. Changing careers is hard. While I don't recommend sending a *Reply All* note when you do it, sometimes you do have to *unsubscribe* from your past to grab hold of the future.

BE PREPARED FOR YOUR NEXT OPPORTUNITY

Looking at your own career you can probably see a similar pattern emerge. You start down a particular path and you don't know if it's the right path until after you get started. You put your destination in your career GPS and then settle in for the ride. But just like a driver listening to turn-by-turn directions, you've got to be paying attention for that moment of clarity, or you'll end up somewhere you don't want to be.

When I was director over the help desk, FedEx had grown through acquisitions and there was a conglomerate of cultures. Soon there was an initiative of culture reshaping across the company. The message was this: We believe that if you put people first, they'll deliver awesome services. That's what makes us profitable.

But with all the companies coming together, our culture was fragmented. So how do we get everybody level-set to a consistent culture? Our company leadership decided to certify certain leaders as Culture Facilitators. Of course, I volunteered. C-4 Leaders bridge the gap. My boss was a former marine sharp-shooter who was not too keen on the my facilitating of what he called "soft stuff." I got a lot of grief about singing kumbaya at staff meetings, but volunteering for this role was what opened the door for me to pivot to HR.

It happened like this. Our CIO was going to deliver a presentation to his leadership team, about 200 people in one auditorium and another 600 streaming live globally. He asked me to kick off the meeting and talk about culture, because I was a director who was certified as a culture facilitator.

He gave me the first ten minutes on stage to set the tone for a room full of IT Leaders. Now, when I speak, I try to create a roller coaster of emotions—from laughing, to thinking, to emotions that pull at the heartstrings. I had the audience on the edge of their seats. After I finished and invited him on stage, his first words to the crowd were: "Note to self. Never follow Chris Winton again."

My whole career changed at that point. The Vice President of HR was sitting in the audience that day, and when she needed an HR person who could speak IT, guess who was on her mind already when I went to talk to her?

You see, C-4 Leaders don't have some special insight that allows them to predict when they'll get their next opportunity to shine. They face the same glass ceiling as everyone else, but what makes them different is how they respond to the heat.

I could have declined the CIO when he asked me to speak, or I could have been paralyzed by the moment and done a terrible job.

But I knew where I wanted to succeed. I had been thinking about it for years. So when the opportunity came, I was ready to seize it.

Do you know where you are going? You need clarity to bring the heat and ignite your career. You need a clear destination before you ever start on your journey. If you want to break through your glass ceiling, be prepared for the heat. Don't run from it. Without it you'll never explode through barriers.

Use that clarity as the catalyst that sparks your success. Without it, you're just driving around—and that's never good.

CHAPTER 4

WHAT'S HOLDING YOU BACK?

THERE'S NO NEED to sugarcoat it. Pressure is painful.

It intrudes on the status quo. It's disruptive. It can make things better or worse, depending on how you respond. But it is often the catalyst you need to move the needle and yield new and better results.

Sometimes we get so entrenched in our ways that we fail to see new options. We stop growing because what we are doing is working—until it isn't. Then comes the pain of pressure. But just like pressure on coal produces a diamond, pressure on the C-4 Leader can yield amazing results.

I know, because it took painful pressure to shape my character and make me into the type of leader who could be trusted to handle the C-4 necessary for growth.

When I got started at FedEx, the Vice President of Technology Services was a man named Larry Netter. Netter was about five feet tall and weighed about 120 pounds. (Actually, if he's reading this now, he's probably barking, "I'm five-three, Winton!")

Netter was in the United States Marine Corps. And you know what they say about Marines—once a Marine, always a Marine. He was an expert marksman and 3X national champion at ranges of a thousand yards. Legend had it that he could hit a quarter from that distance. Netter's mantra was *I'm firm but fair.*

When I was a young manager in Netter's department, a Director's job opened up and I *wanted that job.* If I got it, I would report directly to Netter, so it was no surprise when I learned he would be conducting the interview.

I was excited. Thirty years old at the time, this was the next logical step for me. I felt prepared for the interview in my navy blue suit, crisp white shirt, and red power tie.

To get ready for the big day, I started practicing my presentation in the mirror. It had been drilled into me *not* to say "uh." It was a big thing in communications, so I practiced until my presentation was perfect. I was more prepared than any actor on the Broadway stage.

When the day of the interview arrived, I was ready. I was pumped. I *knew* I was going to get this job. I walked confidently into the room and there was Netter, sitting in a chair. A second vice-president sat beside him. After minimal small talk—did I salute? I can't remember—I launched into my presentation.

When I was practicing in front of my bathroom mirror at home, I had really maximized the acoustics and developed a "professional interview voice." The deep baritone was sure to impress Netter, so I really laid it on thick: "So, here's the direction we're headed and we're going to get everybody on board." I threw in all the buzzwords I could think of—teamwork, people, service, and profit. I monologued for a while, and at the end of my presentation, I hit him with my haymaker: "And *that's* why I'm a great leader."

In my mind I thought I did great, because I didn't say *uh*. Not even once. This job was as good as mine. He didn't give me any feedback then, but by the look on his face, I could tell I'd given him *a lot* to consider.

Netter had a strict policy, if you wanted feedback you had to ask for it. Why? Because he would be brutally honest. So if you can't handle brutally honest feedback, don't ask.

I felt like I already had the job so I scheduled the follow-up in advance. I knocked on his door with a confident rap. He looked up and said, "Sit down, Winton." He never cracked a smile, and his face was unreadable. My butt had barely touched the chair when he laid into me with all the force a Marine could muster, "Well, this was the biggest waste of my time. Clearly, you can see you aren't gonna get this job. I don't know what the hell *that* was, but that *"Superman"* on your chest doesn't work for me. Now, any questions?"

Ouch.

That was the extent of my feedback. Talk about pressure. I felt it ratchet up to almost an unbearable level. Netter must be wondering *who* hired me? The worst part of that day was that as a manager, my office was right outside his. This meant that every day going forward, I had to see him and think about what he was thinking when he saw me sitting there. Not only was I not being promoted, now my VP must be thinking how I even had a job at all.

Since it was a panel interview, I decided to talk to the other vice president and see if he could give me some additional feedback. What he said was a little softer than Netter's Marine Corps feedback, and it stuck with me.

"Whenever I'm interviewing someone for the next level of leadership," he said to me, "I always ask myself, if we're sitting at a bar together, having a beer and I asked these same questions, would I get the same answer? If the answer is no or if I'm unsure, I *never* promote them to the next level."

That response hit me like a sledgehammer. I thought back to my "professional" voice and realized I blew it as soon as I opened my mouth. They wanted to know who I really was, and I had failed to be authentic. I didn't walk around talking like that. In fact, I didn't even know who that guy was. It certainly wasn't me.

I thanked him for his honest feedback and told him I would take it to heart for the next time I got a chance to interview. Unfortunately, that would take another two years.

During that time I went on a journey to answer this question: *Who am I?*

What I discovered is how much my time at INROADS shaped my understanding of leadership and professionalism. They told me how to speak, how to dress, what to eat for lunch, and what not to eat. It was ingrained in me and I started to realize that as important as those things were, that wasn't all there was to me. I was a totally different guy outside of work.

And that made me ask another question: How do the two come together? Because I can't fake it. I can't get to the next level unless they know who I really am.

You can only lead people to the extent that you know yourself and can lead yourself. As painful and embarrassing as that interview process was, it applied the pressure I needed to build my character. It forced me to go on a journey to discover what was stopping me from getting where I wanted to go. As tough as his feedback was, it wasn't Netter that was the problem, it was me.

What's holding you back? It may not be what you think. In fact, it may be *you*.

WHEN PRESSURE IS A GOOD THING

The truth is, I wasn't ready for that job. I could have probably handled it, but I would have been limited in my potential, because I hadn't faced the pressure that leads to character. I had risen through the ranks at FedEx and achieved some of my goals, but I had never faced a disappointment quite like that failed interview.

It would have been easy to blame it on Larry Netter or the color of my skin or my age, and for a while I did. But deep down, I realized that wasn't really the problem. I had some growing to do and Netter's feedback, although harsh and direct, provided the pressure I needed to grow.

When it comes to leadership, character matters. And the leaders who have the deepest character often have the most painful backstories. When you face pressure, you have a choice: *get bitter or get better.*

Getting bitter is easy. It's most people's default mode when things don't go their way. Getting better is hard. It takes character, honesty, and willingness to change and grow. It takes looking yourself in the eye and being honest about where you are falling short. And it takes determination to blow up some things that don't belong to get to the gold underneath.

***

"When it comes to leadership, character matters."

***

Just like explosives, power can't be just handed to anyone. It takes someone with the character to use that power wisely and not only for his or her own advancement or personal gain. It must be used responsibly.

There is a reason you can't just run down to Home Depot and buy C-4. It's highly regulated because not everyone is qualified to use it. Leaders who lack character aren't ready to unlock the potential energy of C-4 Leadership. They need to go through some character-defining moments first.

Nothing builds character like pressure. If you're going to go anywhere in leadership, you cannot be easily detonated. You have to take the pressure and absorb the shock. People are going to drop you. You'll get kicked around. You'll get passed over for promotions.

You'll get dinged in a job review. You have to absorb the impact and pressure and allow it to build your character. It's painful in the moment, but it's the only thing that will set you up to unlock the power of C-4 Leadership.

Remember when I talked about how C-4 detonates? It takes two things. First, it takes a spark. The spark provides the heat needed to start the explosive reaction. The second is the pressure. The spark at the end of the blasting cap is so small that it won't ignite the explosive in the C-4. It would just fizzle out with a puff of smoke. But that spark's job is not to ignite the entire block of C-4, it's job is to ignite the explosive in the blasting cap.

When that happens, it creates the pressure in the form of a small explosion that causes a reaction in the C-4. The pressure from that small explosion is the catalyst that yields a big boom.

Life and leadership is a lot like that.

Each day, week, month, and year, you face small flare-ups of heat. These make you uncomfortable, but they don't always yield a big change. If you have indigestion after a greasy meal, you may have a bout of heartburn, but you probably aren't going to dramatically change your diet. You'll give it a few weeks and then return to the greasy spoon.

If you miss a deadline on a work project, but get it done and suffer few ill-effects from the boss, it may not change the way you schedule your time. You'll deal with the momentary grief you get and press forward.

But ratchet up the pressure, and you get the impetus for change. When that greasy meal leads to an ER trip because you think you're having a heart attack, that pressure can lead to an explosion of change. When the boss notices you missed a deadline and calls you out on it in front of the team, that pressure can lead to an explosion of change.

THE PATH TO PHENOMENAL

Pressure reveals your character. We all face moments of pressure. It comes with life. But what you do in those moments reveals the character deep within. What you *do* is a result of the habits you build up over time. Pressure exposes our habits and makes us examine them in light of where we want to go. Good habits drive you forward. Bad habits hold you back.

In those two years that followed my interview with Netter, I discovered that I had everything I needed to refine who I really was, and become a person of character. I was determined that the next chance I got, I would be ready.

I needed to change some things to alter the course of my career:

- ➤ **THINKING.** I had to adjust from bitter to better. It would have been easy to reject Netter's feedback. But that wouldn't have moved me closer to my goal. So I made it a point to change the way I thought. I chose to see that there were things I could do to improve my ability as a leader and thought about them constantly.

- ➤ **BEHAVIOR.** I began reading leadership books and discovering what great leaders did. But I didn't just copy that. I put it in my own terms. I became the most authentic version of Chris Winton that I could be. This meant becoming comfortable in my own skin and being as close to the same person inside of work as I was outside of work. It was nerve-wracking to put myself out there, but I knew I had to be true to myself before I could lead others.

➤ **HABITS.** The habits I developed as a result of changing my thinking and my behaviors became my touchpoints for success. Habits are external manifestations of internal beliefs. Habits build on each other. I was determined to create the right habits that would lead to exponential improvement.

➤ **RESULTS.** I could sense a change in myself as my character deepened and my authenticity improved. I felt ready for the next opportunity and when it came, I seized it.

PUSHING PRIDE TO THE BACK SEAT

Author James A. Michener wrote, "Character consists of what you do on the third and fourth tries." I had done the work on my character and was ready to try as many times as it took to get where I wanted to go. So, two years after walking out of Netter's office, head hanging, the *same* director's job opened again. Talk about irony.

I put in my application, but this time I had a completely different feeling going in. I decided to just be me. I was just as confident, but this time my confidence was built on my character.

When the day came, I walked into the interview room. Larry Netter was sitting there beside HR and a different VP who smiled as soon as I walked in.

Seeing her smile put me at ease and I thought, *I'm just going to be Chris.* I calmly gave the presentation. I may have even said *uh* once or twice. I said what I had to say and sat down.

I don't even remember much of the interview, but I do remember the last question Larry Netter asked me: "Why are you the right person for this job?"

I paused for a minute and sat back in the chair. I probably felt like an hour went by. Then I began to talk: "If you had asked me that question two years ago, I would've had a perfectly well-scripted answer with five bullets, all starting with the letter *I*."

"But the truth of it now is *I get it,*" I continued. "This actually has nothing to do with me and everything to do with the people I'd be leading." Then I started talking about every manager that was on that team and what value *they* brought to the organization. I shared how, if I could just come into the role and help them all connect the dots, this team could go to the next level.

I was calm and confident, but not cocky. Honestly, I wanted the job, but only if they wanted me—the authentic, true to himself, Chris—to have it. I looked across the table and said, "It's not about me. *That's* why I feel like I'm the right person for the job."

Walking out, I thought, what did I just do? Did I just tell him I'm not the right one? Two of the managers I mentioned were interviewing for the same job, and I was talking *them* up in *my* interview.

C-4 Leadership is all about those kinds of contradictions. I didn't mind talking them up, because I knew I was doing what it took to shatter my glass ceiling. It really didn't matter if they got the job or if I did. I was on the right track and that gave me confidence. I'd survived the pressure of the initial explosion, and it made me stronger.

When the interviews were done, Larry Netter called me into his office. The old ex-Marine still didn't crack a smile. He sat me down and, true to form, gave me brutally honest feedback on where I still needed to improve. But then he said, "Do you still want the job? Because if you do, it's yours."

I had to ask. "After hearing the reasons why I suck, why are you offering me this job?"

He looked at me and said, "You got the job for one reason. You took the feedback. Two years ago when I gave it to you, I wanted to see how you were going to respond. Today, you put other people first and *then* you ended with why you were the right person for the job. I knew you were ready then."

Then he paid me perhaps the highest compliment he could as he looked me in the eye: "I know I can trust you in the trenches."

I thought about what the other VP said about if we were at a bar having a beer, and I remembered one other thing he had shared: "The reason I always wonder if you are being authentic is because, at the next level of leadership, we have to go in the trenches together. We have to fight in battles together. We have to go through wars. And if you're going through war, you want to know the person standing beside you. You got to know who this person is because their character is going to come out at that point. Leading is high-pressure. I don't want to find out who you are when the pressure hits. I want to know before."

As a leader, heat and pressure come with the territory. Used the right way, heat can provide clarity and help you ensure you are going somewhere on purpose. Pressure may be painful at the time but it strengthens your character and helps you discover that what's holding you back may be you.

As we move in the steps of C-4 Leadership, it's important that you take ownership of where you are now and decide where you want to go from here. Everything in your career has led up to this point. If you want to shatter your glass ceiling, you can. It's time to *execute*.

C-1: CONSUME

CHAPTER 5

THINK LIKE A SHAREHOLDER

IF YOU EVER hope to explode through your glass ceiling, you're going to have to learn how to separate good, usable information from the noise.

There's no shortage of information to consume. It's everywhere. Co-workers will gladly give you their opinion. Spend twenty seconds on social media and you'll be drowning in noise. Your leaders will tell you what they think. And if your family is anything like mine, they're never shy about giving their opinions.

If you aren't careful, all the noise can distract you from your purpose. In fact, there are many things you've probably learned in your career that you need to *un*learn if you hope to make it to the top.

Take this one, for example: *It's not what you know, it's who you know.* This little nugget of wisdom is probably parroted more times than you can count inside corporations and businesses. And why not? It sounds logical. After all, networking *is* important. If you don't know the right people, how will you ever progress up the leadership ladder and ultimately to the C-suite?

So with the best of intentions, you play golf with the right people. You're seen at the right events. You attend meetings you have no desire or need to attend. But you do it because you believe that if you don't know the right people, you'll never shatter your glass ceiling.

It's common wisdom, but there's only one problem. *It's not true.*

Think about it—*it's not what you know.* When has that ever been true in your life? Even when you were a kid, you were told to go to school and make good grades. Knowing *something* is what got you the grades. Who you knew was almost irrelevant to the outcome. What you knew was critical. So when did we start thinking it wasn't about what you know but who you know?

Remember, your thinking drives behavior, and your behavior drives results. If you spend time thinking it's not *what* you know but *who* you know, you'll spend most of your time trying to expand your network, while neglecting your personal growth and knowledge.

· ·

"It's not who you know, it's actually who needs to know what you know?"

· ·

Focus on getting to know other people before you even get to know yourself, and you'll always be one step behind. Think like a consumer by treating people like commodities and you'll never build solid connections. Hoard information for your own use, and you'll always be frustrated when it's not enough.

That's why I flipped that saying on its head. It's not *who you know,* it's actually *who needs to know what you know?* What if you weren't just meeting people at a networking event for the sake of meeting, but you became a person who brought incredible value to those people?

Imagine sharing insights about something they are interested in. Imagine sharing information that leads to a solution to a problem they are facing. Imagine being the person in the room that *everyone* wants to talk to because you leave them feeling empowered, encouraged, and engaged.

That kind of meeting of the minds is what happens when iron sharpens iron. The next time you meet someone new, this perspective shifts your aim. You start to think, "What do I have of value to give them? What insights can I share that will help contribute to them in some way?"

You stop thinking quid pro quo and start thinking, "How can I help?"

In your organization, who needs to know what you know? It's the difference between thinking like a consumer and thinking like a shareholder. A consumer is self-focused and looks for the benefit the organization can bring them. A shareholder is outward-focused and looks for the benefit they can bring to the organization.

If you want to become a C-4 Leader, you've got to turn your thinking inside out. But before you can share what you know with others, you've got to make sure what you know is what they need to know.

Confused yet? Don't worry, we'll walk through this together, but know this: your *inputs* determine your *outputs*. Consume the wrong info and what you know won't matter. Consume the right info and what you know can change your life, leadership, and impact in the organization.

BE CAREFUL WHERE YOU GET YOUR INPUTS

I love my dad. He's one of the greatest influences on my life. At the time of this writing, he's 66 years old. I've learned so many things from his life—watching him work hard, achieve his version of success, and take care of his family.

Sometimes he teaches me lessons without even meaning to.

One day we were talking and, almost in an offhand way, he said, "If I knew then what I know now...." You've probably heard people say that; you may have even said it yourself. For whatever reason, what he said really hit me hard. I asked him to explain.

He said he meant that if his 40-year-old self could have access to his 66-year-old wisdom, things would have been different. The reason it stood out to me is because I remember my 40-year-old dad saying things to the 22-year-old me. When he said those things back then, he didn't seem at all uncertain. In fact, he seemed to be speaking powerfully with hard-earned wisdom. He didn't seem to doubt anything he was telling me.

But now, I realized that what he believed then may have changed. His core beliefs remain unchanged, but what he believed to be true at the time looks different with the benefit of hindsight. It struck me even more that when my dad was my age, there was no internet or as much access to information, so his inputs were more managed by others.

Even so, as he looked back, he realized he didn't know it all.

Much of my thinking today is grounded on what my dad taught me then. I realized that with the benefit of hindsight, things can look much different. It's what forced me to reevaluate *it's not what you know, it's who you know.* Sometimes things are so deeply rooted in you that you never stop to question why you believe what you believe. Or, like me, you trust the source without ever verifying the information.

If you want to become a C-4 Leader, you've got to be willing to reexamine some things and possibly *change your mind.* Just because you thought something twenty-five years ago or you heard somebody you respect say it, doesn't always mean it's true. The world has shifted and your inputs need to shift with it.

Be careful where you get your inputs. They go much deeper in shaping your thinking than you may realize.

A SHAREHOLDER MINDSET

One of the greatest compliments I've ever received was in a performance review. It was not long after I became a vice president, but as soon as I read it, I knew it had been true for my whole career. My boss at the time wrote these words: *Chris thinks like a shareholder.*

It's a simple statement, but it perfectly sums up my work ethic. Whether at Dan's Big Star, or INROADS, or FedEx, I do my best to treat each job as more than a job. This mindset is deeply ingrained in my thinking.

That performance review was the first time I'd heard myself described that way. Of course, I knew the term *shareholder.* It's hard to work for a Fortune 100 company and *not* know the term. But usually it's directed outward. It's reserved for the people who *didn't* work for a Fortune 100 and expected us, as employees, to make a good return on their investments.

When I heard her say those words to me, something clicked. It's so easy to define yourself by your role or title. For many years, I thought of myself as an IT guy. It's what I knew. I was proud of all I had accomplished in that field, but limiting myself to thinking I was just an IT guy would limit all of my thinking. At FedEx, we're all in the business of moving packages. This is as true now that I'm in HR as it was when I was in IT.

Thinking like a shareholder causes you to look beyond your title. You think big picture and you do what it takes to make everyone around you successful.

You also set yourself up for success. How? By making sure you consume the right kind of information. Shareholders focus on what is important and ignore what isn't. They make sure they consume the right knowledge to impact their decisions. They ensure that what they know is beneficial to others and become an asset across the organization.

Thinking like a shareholder enables me to connect the dots across teams, divisions, and areas of responsibility. It equips me to engage in meaningful conversation with different people even though we may have little in common.

In most organizations, people don't do that. They stay head-down in their own little area of expertise. They do *their job* and that's all. They're like an old mule with blinders on, blindly trudging forward and wondering why they are so unfulfilled.

I love IT, so I'm not picking on them, but I saw this happen time and again in that field. Software developers have one job—develop code. To a software developer, if you write good code that performs according to spec, you've succeeded. But in any organization, code has a bigger purpose than just working. It's part of the bigger business picture.

If you can understand a little bit about the lifecycle of software development, you can see why this is important. It usually goes something like this. The business person writes the requirements: *I need the software to do X.* They hand over those requirements to the software developer who sits in a room for six months, develops everything according to the requirements, and then gives it back to the business leader.

Once it's put into effect, the business leader tests it out to see if it has the desired outcome. There's always a constant tension between IT and business. If the business side doesn't get the results they *expected,* they go back to the software developer. If the developer isn't thinking like a shareholder, they'll push back. After all, they designed the code according to specifications, so in their eyes they've succeeded. It may work as designed, but does it work as *desired?*

That's what I think happens in the corporate world a lot of times. People say, "Hey, I nailed my part of the process." And while that may be true, if it doesn't lead to the desired outcome for the organization, you can't call it a success.

A shareholder always asks, how healthy is the organization as a whole? They look beyond their small part to the bottom line. These questions guide them: Am I delivering on the bottom-line target? Did all the components come together to deliver the goal? What can I do to improve the entire system?

The person that understands *how* will always have a job, but the person that understands *why* will be the leader. It sounds like the start of a joke, but when IT, marketing, sales, and engineering work together to define the overall goal, they can make great progress *together* working on their individual parts. They componentize things into their job, and do their job with excellence. This process requires a mental shift.

The guy that knows how to dig a ditch will always have a job. The person that understands why he's digging this ditch will be the boss. Thinking like a shareholder moves you from ditch-digger to something more. How do IT, marketing, sales, and the engineer execute on their individual responsibilities, while working together to achieve the ultimate goal?

By thinking like a shareholder.

When you look up, look out, and become intentional about learning the other components of the organization, you become an invaluable asset. And when the need arises for *what you know,* and the right people know what you know, amazing things can happen.

WHO KNOWS WHAT YOU KNOW?

Shortly after I became the new VP of HR, the Chief HR Officer sent me a message. She was going to be out of town and needed me to sit in for her in Fred Smith's staff meeting. My stomach did a nervous flip, but I quickly became excited. This was the chance I'd been waiting for.

Then she handed me the pre-meeting briefing which I was expected to study before the meeting. It landed on my desk with an audible thud. I'm not kidding when I say it was at least 100 pages long. And the meeting was in a few days.

I swallowed and asked, "Are they expecting me to read *all* of this?"

She smiled and said, "Yes, you need to read it all."

As she was walking out my door she told me one more thing: "Chris, you need to understand something. Fred Smith *will* read the entire report. Not only that, he'll have read every page and he can tell you page 26 doesn't align with page 82 because the numbers are off. So study it and be prepared, because you are the voice of HR at that table."

She walked out. I immediately went into cramming mode.

Days later, I walked into the executive boardroom. I got there nice and early. I knew Fred is former military so punctuality would be appreciated. Besides I already felt a little out of place. I didn't want to add a fashionably late entrance to my discomfort.

Looking around at the assigned seats, it felt like I was joining a table of generals or something. My brain was racing, "Oh crap, don't sit in the wrong seat, Winton!" I quickly found my place at the table and sat down. It didn't take long for the rest of the people to come in and take their seats.

When the Chairman walked in and sat at the head of the table, I couldn't remember what protocol was. *Do I stand? Salute? Bow? Kiss the ring?*

Unfortunately, I went right back to my old way of thinking—*I'm not supposed to be here.* My parents worked in the Hub at night. No one's ever told me what to do in these moments. *They don't want me here anyway. I'm the only black guy in the room. I'm younger than everyone else.*

As these things were ricocheting in my mind, Fred Smith looked up from his papers with a bit of a scowl on his face. His eyes landed on me. He stood up, walked past the CFO, slid by other leaders, and headed straight towards me. I started to stand up, but he said, "No, stay seated. Welcome, Chris."

He walked back to the head of the table, sat down and said, "All right, now we can get started." Immediately, my heart calmed. That simple interaction made a huge impression on me. Fred Smith, the CEO of FedEx, made it a point to know who I was and come over to introduce himself. Suddenly, I felt like an equal at the table.

It boosted my confidence as I felt I could contribute to this conversation because I had taken the time to consume the right information. For the next six hours, we discussed the details of that one-hundred page briefing.

In a meeting like that, you don't just talk surface level, you dive deep. I had always prided myself on being able to connect the dots and see things others couldn't see, but this was next level. I was so glad I had read through that report and prepared. Once you get a seat at the table, you have to make sure you've consumed the right information. That day, *who* I knew didn't matter at all; *what* I knew was critical.

At that table, I brought what I knew. To Fred Smith, I was the expert on the labor market. Our business is moving packages, but packages don't move without people. So when he asked a question about the forty-thousand package handlers in the ground division, I was ready to answer.

I could have walked out of that meeting bragging that I "knew" Fred Smith. He walked over to me, shook my hand, and called me by name. If I had believed that who I know was all that mattered, I would have been all set. But I realized it was more than that.

From my seat at that table, I was able to show Fred Smith *what* I knew. The CEO of FedEx now knew what I knew. That was more important to me than any bragging rights.

YOU'RE GOING TO NEED TISSUES FOR THIS

That reminds me of something that happened not long after I'd become director over the IT Help Desk. A young lady from my department asked to speak with me. She worked the help desk on the third shift and, for some reason, she wanted to skip past her manager and meet with me one-on-one. I had an open-door policy, so I had my assistant schedule the meeting.

On the day of the appointment, I could hear her power heels clicking against the floor as she walked down the hall. She walked into my office decked out with high-end clothes, tall red heels, and sparkly jewelry. I thought she looked very put-together for a third-shift help desk worker, but I was determined to give her the time I had promised.

I offered her a seat and asked her how I could help. She took a deep breath and sort of exhaled-spoke-vented all at once: "Well, I just wanted you to know that I respect the chain of command, that's why I wanted to tell you first. But I know you probably can't do anything at your level, so you'll need to talk to your boss."

Okay, this should be interesting. I kept my poker face and listened as she continued.

She went on to tell me that what we were paying her was beneath her. She had talked to several of her friends and family who couldn't believe how we were taking advantage of her. She had waited eight months to see if we were going to do something about it, but now she was insulted, because we hadn't done anything about this alleged injustice.

Apparently, she took my stunned silence as an invitation to keep going: "I mean, I have a Master's degree. I have ten years of experience with four different Fortune 100 companies. For y'all to be paying me this, and keeping me in the job you've got me in is insulting."

Speaking of insulting, her next words blew me away: "Now, I understand in your job"—she waved her hand dismissively at me—"you're going to need to talk to your boss. So just tell me whatever you need from me to make something happen."

Well, I had to give her credit for having the—a-hem, *gumption* to walk into my office, take a seat at my table, and unload on me with both barrels. That took courage. Or confidence. Or something. But unfortunately, I knew this wasn't going to end well for her.

I got up from my chair, walked behind my desk, and grabbed a box of tissues from the shelf. I walked back to the table where she was sitting and sat the box down in front of her.

She looked up and said, "What are those for?"

"You're going to need those in a minute."

I sat back down and said, "Now, you've had an opportunity to be honest and candid with me, correct? I'd like the same opportunity to be candid with you."

I asked her if I could ask a few questions. She agreed.

First, I asked, "What is my vision for this organization?"

She looked puzzled and didn't answer.

"That's okay," I smiled, nodding, "not everybody knows the vision. What is the mission here? What do we show up every day to accomplish?

Again, silence.

"Again, that's okay, because I just covered these in the town hall meeting two weeks ago. I also covered four strategic focus areas. Can you give me two of them?"

Crickets.

"How about just one?"

No response.

I let the silence fill the room for a moment and then said, "So you don't know the strategic focus areas. Okay. What are *your* objectives for the year?"

Apparently, she had fully consumed the belief from her friends and family that we were taking advantage of her brilliance. She'd memorized her opening shot, but had little else to add. She couldn't name her own objectives.

I looked her in the eye and said, "So let me get this straight. You don't know the vision or where we're headed. You don't know the mission and what we're showing up to accomplish every day. You don't know any of the strategic focus areas to get us to that destination. How is your Master's degree and your ten years of experience supposed to help me?"

"And why am I supposed to pay you for it?" I was on a roll. "Your degree and education mean nothing to me if it doesn't add value to what we're trying to accomplish as an organization. Stop thinking people are going to pay you for it. You just consumed a lot of information for your own benefit. Honestly, I'm still trying to figure out how you got the job."

(Oh man, I was turning into Netter!)

Judging from the shocked look on her face, this may have been the first time anyone ever spoke that level of truth to her. She wasn't thinking like a shareholder. She wasn't looking at what she could do for FedEx, she was looking at what FedEx could do for her.

After she offered up some excuses for why she didn't make it to the town hall meeting, I said, "So you didn't show up at the town hall meeting to consume the information about where we were going. You didn't even read the email I sent you. And you didn't spend any energy to talk to me about how your expertise and education will help achieve those objectives. But you actually expect somebody to pay you for it?"

It took a moment for that to sink in. Then she reached for the tissues.

Unfortunately, that's the way it is with many people. They expect to be paid for their education, but they don't contribute. They want a seat at the table, but haven't prepared for when they get there. Their career is all about *me, me, me*, and then they wonder why no one wants to help them.

That's not thinking like a shareholder. And that's why those kinds of people stay stuck right where they are. They aren't stable. They aren't moldable. They don't have personal or professional clarity. They don't respond well to pressure. So when the time comes to ignite or burn out, they just fizzle out.

WHAT ARE YOU CONSUMING?

When it comes to what you consume, your thinking is key. Think like a victim or a person who is only out for themselves and you'll seek inputs that reinforce those beliefs. Think like a shareholder, and you'll look at the bigger picture. You'll seek inputs that connect the dots and make you an asset when you do get your seat at the table.

Your thinking drives your behavior. Your behavior is what people see when they evaluate you and what determines your results. Consume the right information, put it into practice each day, and you'll change your results. Change your results, and you change your future.

As you evaluate your ability to think like a shareholder, consider these questions:

➤ What are you currently consuming? How is it helping you draw closer to your goals?

➤ If you were asked to take a seat at the table, how would you know you are prepared?

➤ What do you need to *un*learn to reach your potential?

➤ What do you need to change to begin thinking like a shareholder?

➤ What do you know that sets you apart from everyone else?

➤ Who needs to *know* what you know?

When you decide to take charge of your leadership, it unlocks your potential. You stop making excuses and start making things happen. And before long, people notice. And when the right people notice, you start to feel like you belong.

CHAPTER 6

YOUR LEADERSHIP CRAFT

YOU CAN FORM a bad habit—or at least a habit that doesn't add anything to your life—almost by accident. In his bestselling book, *Atomic Habits: An Easy & Proven Way to Build Good Habits & Break Bad Ones,* James Clear defines a habit as "a routine or practice performed regularly; an automatic response to a specific situation."

When it comes to what you consume, your habits may drive more than you think. When I discovered this in my own life, it was so eye-opening that it changed how I began my day.

Several years ago, I used to really be into witchcraft.

Now before you start judging me, let me explain, because it's not what you think. Do you remember the television show *Charmed*? It was the story of three sisters who lived in San Francisco and discovered that, while they looked and acted like regular women, they were actually powerful witches. The good thing is, they were good witches who used their power to fight evil.

Like many people, I have the habit of turning on the TV when I get ready for work. My go-to show back then? *Charmed.* Now I wasn't kicking back on the couch and settling in for the whole show, but I would listen to it in the background as I got ready.

Good? Bad? I can't really say. It's just a show. It didn't add anything to my life or make me a better person, it was just something to listen to as I moved around the house.

As I moved up in my career track, I started to feel like I didn't have as much time as I needed to get everything done. It was frustrating. I looked at the successful people I knew; they had the same twenty-four hours as I did, so how did they do it all with their crazy schedules?

I realized that they must have different habits. Perhaps their habits started in the morning. I immediately thought of my friendly witches Piper, Phoebe, and Paige. Sure, they kept me company in the morning, but they weren't teaching me much I could use in my job.

Not long after that, my friend and business coach, Anthony Flynn, walked me through an exercise called Plan 168. It opened my eyes to how much time I was wasting. I actually had *40 hours per week* that I couldn't account for. I knew I felt crazy busy and had been telling myself I didn't have enough time to consume anymore. But by looking at my typical week—when I worked, ate, slept, spent time with the kids, went on a date with my wife—I discovered that *I did* have room to consume things that would improve my leadership.

The key is identifying that automatic response and putting it to work. It would just take some willpower and modification of my daily routine.

The next morning, I said goodbye to the three witches of *Charmed* and hello to *Squawk Box* on CNBC. That day, and just about every day after, I heard FedEx mentioned at least once in the morning news. The company is a leading indicator of economic health, so I started to listen. As I did, I let that information soak into my subconscious.

It was a very small change. I got up at the same time. I kept the same routine. I didn't make any huge sacrifices. I simply changed the channel and modified what I was consuming. But that small change yielded powerful results.

When I went into a staff meeting, I could talk more confidently about the labor market. I had the same information as Fred Smith.

I could anticipate the questions he would ask and have an insightful answer ready.

Because of those mornings watching CNBC, I picked up on a trend. I kept hearing the talk about Baby Boomers retiring, and how the market was heading for full employment. In those meetings, it seemed like I was able to predict the future. It wasn't witchcraft, it was connecting the dots.

We were heading into a war for talent. But because I was making time to consume the right things, I was ready to fight that war.

MAXIMIZE YOUR TIME

It's easy to buy into the lie that you don't have time. Time is the only resource you can never get more of, so it naturally feels limited. Like me and every other person, you probably waste a good deal of time on things that don't matter.

The hard truth is, we all make time for what is important to us. If you love football, you will spend hours in front of the television watching your team play. If you love golf, you have a set tee time each weekend. If you have a close group of friends, you meet for coffee each week.

Time is the great limiter. You, Bill Gates, Jeff Bezos, Fred Smith, your neighbor down the street, and the doctor working to find a cure for cancer *all* have twenty-four hours in their day, 168 hours in their week.

When it comes to time, it's not the quantity; it's the quality that counts. What you choose to do with those hours is critical.

C-4 Leaders don't make excuses—they make things happen. They evaluate where they spend their time and maximize their efforts on things that matter. They monitor what they consume and optimize its impact on their leadership growth. They recognize that to succeed, they have to say *no* to the things that aren't as important, so they can say *yes* to the things that are.

We all make time for what we want to pursue. The question is, are you pursuing what's important or are you letting your weeks just drift by? The Plan 168 exercise (see the end of the chapter) forced me to get clear about these things:

➤ What gives me the most self-fulfillment?

➤ What gives me the least self-fulfillment?

➤ What would the people who know me the best say lights me up?

➤ What would the people who know me the best say drains me?

Once I thought through these questions, I began to think about my time. I thought about these five domains: personal, family, church, career, and community. Then I looked at how *much* time I was spending in each of these areas. It didn't take long to notice some patterns that were working against me.

Don't get me wrong. Everyone needs down time. You need time to relax and unwind. But like anything in life, you can take this to the extreme. If you binge-watch your way through life, you'll never get where you want to go. Finding balance between what you *have to do* and what you *want to do* is key. Adding things to your life that add value to your goals is the secret that unlocks your potential.

THE CRAFT OF LEADERSHIP

In his 2008 book *Outliers,* Malcolm Gladwell introduced the 10,000 hour rule. It states that if you spend 10,000 hours working towards a craft, you will become an expert in that craft. There have been several studies that have questioned the veracity of this claim, but one thing is true: you'll never become great at anything without a lot of practice.

Kobe Bryant would practice four times a day when the average player would practice twice. He figured out how to give his body just enough rest to go back at it again in order to get to that 10,000 hours. Michael Jordan would shoot 1,000 free throws every day. In the off-season, NFL receivers and quarterbacks hold private workout sessions to practice running routes and making catches.

Leadership, like athletics, is a craft. There are no born leaders. You have to study and work at leadership if you hope to improve. When I started focusing on the *craft* of leadership by reading John Maxwell and Peter Drucker, it changed my thinking. And that changed my behavior.

I no longer drifted through my day. I was an active participant, looking for leadership lessons all day, every day.

When you develop a leadership awareness, you start to see lessons in the leaders you interact with. It fascinated me to go into establishments where everyone was dressed the same and try to pick out the leader. The leader always stood out.

I believe we are drawn to people who have that look. There is something in their bearing that says, "I know where I'm going, and I'd like you to follow." If you start looking for leaders—in your office, in your building, at your church, or at the mall—you'll find them. Their lessons can guide you.

Yet unlike a sport, where you can easily count your progress, leadership has to become instinctive and automatic. You know when you've shot 1,000 free throws; your tired arms will remind you. But how many books read or conferences attended make you a leader? If you're keeping score that way, you're going to be disappointed. Just as heaving a basketball in the general direction of the goal won't make you a great free-throw shooter, simply consuming leadership information won't make you a great leader.

If you study the greats, *they don't count.* To them, looking for leadership lessons becomes habit forming. It becomes a part of everything they are and everything they do. They start to view the world differently.

If I were to just watch a leader, say Fred Smith, in action, would I become a better leader by default? Kind of like leadership by osmosis? Of course, the answer is *no.* Just being around a great leader won't *make* you a great leader.

The reason is simple—you are unique. And as a unique person, you'll need to grow in unique ways. You may need to consume something that I've already mastered. I may need to consume something that comes naturally to you. Your leadership needs will determine how you approach the craft.

When Tiger Woods hurt his back, he had to re-engineer his swing. His putting was fine, but when he wanted to drive the ball from the tee he had to adapt to his new limitations. When he did, he began winning again. As Michael Jordan got older, he mastered the fadeaway jumper and worked on his three point shooting. Any athlete knows where to focus because they enlist a coach to speak objectively to them.

As a C-4 Leader, you should also enlist a coach, but you must also develop self-awareness that serves as your guide. Ask yourself, *What do I need to learn about leadership based on what I've seen in me so far?* When you are honest about where you struggle, you can create a plan to improve.

NEVER FORGET THE PURPOSE OF LEADERSHIP

A word of caution here.

When I started to watch other leaders and learn from them, read leadership books, and hone the craft of my leadership, I didn't forget one thing—leadership is all about people.

I don't want you to misunderstand me and think that working on your leadership craft is all about *taking* from others. It's not. It's about learning *from* others so you replicate what works and avoid what doesn't. It's not selfish in the sense that you are learning just for yourself. It's learning so you can be a better leader to people.

I've had both good and bad leaders. To be honest, I've taken away just as much from the bad as I have the good. When leadership is your craft, you file it away as something to avoid.

When I became the Director of the Help Desk, I learned a valuable lesson about the real purpose of leadership. My friend Kim, who worked with me at the grocery store in high school and started with me at FedEx, was now my technical lead.

She came to me one day and said, "Chris, I'm ready to go into management. Will you help me?"

Of course I wanted to help her, so I asked her to pitch in on several projects. We were looking at consolidating all of the help desk because we had acquired different companies. I asked Kim to take the lead. But I warned her, "It's going to wear you out. You're going to work like crazy, but I've got your back. Just let me know what you need."

She excitedly said, "I'm in. Let's do it."

Kim jumped in with both feet and took complete ownership of the project. She was cranking it out, sometimes eighty hours a week. But I began to sense something wasn't quite right. Every time I'd ask if she was okay, she'd say, "I'm fine. I'm fine. Let's go!"

We kept running into all kinds of obstacles on the project. Each one seemed to take more of a toll on Kim. When I pressed her on how she was doing, she admitted to me that she had gone to the doctor for some health issues, but wanted to keep going. After talking to her manager, we decided to add another project manager. It balanced the load but couldn't take all the stress away.

The project took eighteen months, but we finally got it across the finish line. We had a big celebration planned at an offsite location in another city, so we had chartered a corporate jet. I was so excited for Kim! She'd led this project magnificently and deserved the chance to shine. I told her, "Kim, this is your moment. I want you sitting up front on the plane, right next to the executive in charge!"

The celebration was scheduled for Thursday. The jet would be taking off at 9 A.M. But on Tuesday of that week, Kim didn't show up to work. I got a call from her mom later that morning. She had passed out at home and been rushed to the hospital. I went to visit her after work that day, but she had slipped into a coma. I was deeply worried about my friend and let her mom know that we'd be praying for her. She promised to let me know if there was anything I could do.

On Thursday morning when we flew out for the event, Kim's seat was conspicuously empty. I was saddened that she couldn't be there to celebrate all of her hard work. After we flew back, I went to the hospital to check on Kim. There had been no change in her condition. The doctors weren't sure what to do.

By Monday morning, I learned the sad news—my friend Kim had passed away. She was only thirty-five years old. At her funeral, her fiancé came up to me and said words I'll never forget: "She just kept saying every day that she didn't want to let you down."

That crushed me. She had spent the last eighteen months of her life working all of those hours to not let *me* down.

At my next performance review, my boss made an offhand remark, "That was good work on the help desk consolidation process, but we need to move you to something else. Nobody really cares about the help desk."

I couldn't help but think of Kim.

"I know one person that really cared, and she gave her life for it."

I never looked at my boss the same again. Maybe he didn't know how much Kim meant to me. Maybe he didn't care. All I know is he forgot the simple fact: leadership is about people.

WHAT TO DO WHEN YOU CAN'T DO IT ALL

Like my friend Kim, it can be easy to think you have to do it all. But it's just not possible. You can't be all things for all people. You can't consume every leadership book. You can't endlessly attend seminars or workshops. You've still got a life to live and a job to do. So how do you decide what to consume and where to focus?

In school, obviously your major focus is studying for your education. Graduate, and your job becomes your focus. Get married and have kids, and now you've got a family to care for. Before long, you're on autopilot, giving little thought to your personal development. Wake up, get dressed, get everyone out the door, commute, put in your work day, commute again, ask what's for dinner, help the kids with homework, go to bed, sleep, wake up.

Tomorrow? You do it all again.

I used to say that I needed an eighth day in the week or a twenty-eight hour day to get it all done, but my friend Anthony challenged my thinking. He laughed, "Man, you still think you've got a time management problem. Actually you have an *energy*-management problem."

"Nothing is neutral."

I'm going to challenge you in the same way he challenged me. You may think time-management is the problem when what you actually have is an energy problem. The things you consume either energize or de-energize you. Nothing is neutral.

When I thought time was my problem, working through the Plan 168 exercise helped me see that I actually had plenty of time—in fact, I discovered those *forty wasted hours* during each week. It's not that I wasn't busy during those forty hours; rather, I was busy wasting those hours.

Anthony and I sat down one day with a blank sheet of paper. He began to ask me questions. He said that every time he did this exercise with someone, they discovered a whole block of time they weren't maximizing. For me it was watching *Charmed* in the mornings and all the March Madness basketball games or the football games between teams I don't even like.

He then challenged me to stop thinking, *I'm going to take away from my family if I focus on me.* You can still make time for what's important—whether it's family time, hobbies, or leisure time. The key is to minimize wasted time and build in time for what's important.

As I reprioritized my time, something incredible dawned on me. I could apply those forty available hours per week to developing my leadership craft. Those extra forty hours per week added up to *2,000 hours* over the course of the year. If I seriously applied myself to developing my craft, in five years I would reach the 10,000 hour mark!

You may be thinking, "Sure, Chris, that's fine for you, but I'm just too busy to do all that." Not to be harsh, but if you are too busy to spend time on personal growth and development, you'll never shatter the glass ceiling in your life. And it's not as difficult as you think. When you find something that intrigues you—that pushes you to be better—you'll pursue it with all you're worth.

As you start to look for leadership lessons, it won't take long until you find them everywhere. You are retraining your brain to pull information and apply it to your life. So when you see a leader acting with integrity, you file it away. When you read a leadership book, you mark down the quotes and lessons you learn. When you listen to a podcast on your commute, you take down the information that applies to where you are.

Separately, all these things can seem disconnected, but put together join up like links in a chain. When you need an example, you have plenty to choose from. When you want someone to model your leadership after, you've learned from the best. And when you're serious about growing as a leader, you have all the raw data you need to put it together.

If you are serious about your leadership craft, here are some places you can start:

➤ **PODCASTS.** Find podcasts that teach leadership lessons. Look for things that are different than what you normally consume so they push you to see things differently.

➤ **BOOKS.** Read books about leadership principles.
  ○ *Developing the Leader Within You,* JOHN MAXWELL
  ○ *The Tipping Point,* MALCOLM GLADWELL
  ○ *The Traveler's Gift,* ANDY ANDREWS
  ○ *The Execution Pipeline,* ANTHONY FLYNN

➤ **SEMINARS/WORKSHOPS.** Attend seminars and workshops that teach you new approaches to leadership.

➤ **CONFERENCES.** Participate in conferences and take notes on speakers who you identify with. Follow up by reading and consuming their material.

➤ **TED TALKS.** Search for TED Talks that look at leadership in a different, often thought-provoking light.

When you get serious about your growth you'll discover that there is no shortage of material to consume. The trick will be creating a process to consume it and connecting the dots about what you learn. That's what C-2 Connect is all about.

WHAT ARE YOUR LEADERSHIP CONSUMPTION HABITS?

Habits happen whether we mean for them to or not. Sometimes we can drift into habits (as I did with *Charmed*) that aren't bad, but that don't help get you where you want to go. When you understand that leadership is a craft that must be developed, it allows you to view everything you do with greater clarity. Once you know where you want to go, you can work hard to eliminate anything that stands in your way.

As you evaluate your leadership as a craft, consider these questions:

➤ What are you consuming?

➤ Does it help or hurt your leadership growth?

➤ How do you spend your 168 hours per week?

➤ How important are the people you lead to you?

➤ Are you discovering more so you can add more value to them?

➤ What are you learning this month? This week? Today?

➤ Who needs to know what you know? Are you sharing it?

When you get clear on what you know, what you don't, and how to close the gap between the two, it becomes an exciting adventure. The answers you need are out there; it's up to you to go find them and apply them to your life and leadership.

C-2: CONNECT

CHAPTER 7

YOU SEE DOTS, I SEE CONNECTION

HAVE YOU EVER lost your purse or your wallet? It's a panicky feeling to lose money. Your mind goes into overdrive. You try to retrace your steps. You take a mental inventory of everything that was inside. *How much cash were you carrying? What credit cards were in there? Maybe a good Samaritan will find it and track you down to return it.* On and on it goes.

Losing money is never fun; especially when you work so hard to make it in the first place.

But what if it wasn't the small amount of cash in your wallet or purse. What if it was something more that you lost. A lot more. *Like one million dollars.* How would that make you feel?

And what if instead of a one-time loss of a million dollars (which would be bad enough), you were losing *a million dollars a minute?*

Is your heart racing yet? Mine got there in a hurry not long after I became Director of IT Operations. My job was to create a global command center, a 24/7 watch to keep an eye out for problems and implement solutions.

By that time, I'd been in IT for nearly fifteen years. Everybody knew me, from the CIO down to the interns. I was at ease and felt completely qualified to do the job well. Most days it was business as usual.

So, it was alarming to get the call at midnight saying, "Chris, we've got a system outage." All systems were down. Nobody knew why. They couldn't locate the problem but it was catastrophic. All flights were grounded, which meant that *over six hundred* FedEx planes were sitting on runways around the world. They were loaded with freight, but unable to move.

When you ship over 10 million packages every day, data is your friend. I knew that if our planes didn't take off within a specific time window, we'd quickly begin losing money. How much? It worked out to roughly *a million dollars a minute.*

You've probably heard the saying, "Culture eats strategy for lunch." Well, that night, it was about to eat breakfast and dinner, too. When it's go-time, and all of the pressure is on, you find out the character of each person—yourself included.

WELCOME TO THE PRESSURE COOKER

Have you ever experienced a crisis like this? Maybe a mistake on your watch didn't ground a fleet of planes, but everyone has faced a situation where things quickly escalated out of control. Maybe you lost your biggest customer because of a simple error. Perhaps you overlooked the competition, and they made huge inroads into your market. Maybe you said something in a meeting that has never been forgotten and seems to have derailed your career.

Mistakes are embarrassing. They ratchet up the pressure. They make you feel frustrated because you knew better. They can make you feel inadequate, like maybe you *aren't* the best person for the job. Mistakes—even though they happen to everyone—can leave you feeling incompetent.

And that's a feeling no one likes.

Pressure reveals a lot about your character and how you think. What comes out on the other side can either cripple you or propel you onward and upward. Like C-4, pressure can either be molded and shaped to redirect the impact or it can blow up and leave you as a pile of wreckage.

When the systems went down that night, we had a protocol in place. I immediately jumped on a conference bridge call with two or three hundred people, trying to control the situation. At the start of the call, in frustration because nothing we were doing seemed to work, someone blurted out, "Who's the idiot running this?" As you can imagine, it was chaos.

As the leader, I was supposed to know exactly who to call and what to do. Everyone was looking at me. But I felt outmatched by my circumstances. Unfortunately, I was not ready for that moment, because I couldn't quickly identify the key people who could provide a quick solution.

If you could have seen me, you'd probably have seen smoke pouring out of my ears; the wheels in my head were turning that quickly. I started thinking of everyone I knew—their backgrounds, their education. I thought of a person strong in computer engineering and asked him to weigh in. He didn't know either.

Meanwhile, the minutes were ticking by, and like a taxi meter spinning away, the costs were rising.

After (wrongly) identifying several people who couldn't help at all, people on the call started throwing out names. *What about Bill? Where's Mike? Sean will know what to do.*

Looking back on that night, it was like I experienced an out-of-body experience. I can still see myself on that call. As they were calling out these names, I recall thinking, *Wait, Sean doesn't even have a degree. What can he do to help? Mike's not even in that department. What are they thinking?*

But as I kept hearing the same names over and over, a light bulb lit up. It was an Aha! Moment for me. In the middle of the chaos, I had a revelation. When the pressure is on, your degree, education, awards, or the size of your office doesn't matter.

All that matters is this: *Can you deliver?*

Once I recognized that the same handful of names kept popping up, I realized they could help us stop the bleeding and avert disaster. We got them on the line and quickly found a solution. Twenty minutes later we had the systems back online. Thanks to people who previously hadn't even been on my radar, the planes were now back in the air and we were shipping packages again.

"All that matters is this: Can you deliver?"

I hung up the phone and slowly sat back down in my desk chair.

As I let out a deep breath and waited for my heart rate to calm down, I thought about the question—*Who's the idiot running this?*

I didn't like the answer, because it was me. I was the idiot in charge.

I was supposed to be the calm voice on the line. In crisis mode, I was supposed to know exactly who to call and what to do. But this time, I didn't. I had thought of the wrong people, while clearly overlooking the right ones.

It seemed I had been consuming the information to make me a great leader, but I had failed to connect the dots. I had some work to do.

THINK LIKE AN ENTREPRENEUR

Entrepreneurs, by definition, think differently. They often see things in a non-traditional manner. That's what makes their success so great. Think about Steve Jobs, Bill Gates, or Mark Zuckerberg. Each dropped out of college to create something that didn't yet exist. If you judged them solely based on their education, you might consider them failures.

But chances are you've already used at least one of the goods or services they created today.

To be clear, I'm not advocating dropping out of college. I am saying that what you learn through experience, success, failure, trial, and error *after* college is where your real education begins.

It turns out that after losing $20 million, you get your butt chewed out pretty badly. Once I could sit down again, I wrote a list of the names I'd heard on that call. I realized that they were the same ten people whose names came up all the time. These "same ten people" or STP had diverse backgrounds, yet they had connected the dots when I could only watch things blow up. They were the men and women who got things done.

I began reaching out to them to see if I could discover why they were so successful. As you might imagine, they were more than happy to help. I started spending as much of my time with them as possible and learning everything about them that I could. As I learned about their backgrounds, I became even more fascinated by their abilities.

One had a biology degree. One had no degree. Another had a degree in electronics but wasn't doing anything in that space. Yet these were the experts running a multi-billion dollar IT ecosystem that launched over 600 planes into the air every night.

The thing I discovered as I learned what made them tick is that they all *thought like entrepreneurs.* They didn't care about their title or their degree or their job description. It's why they were more than willing to talk to me, the guy who was supposed to know it all. They cared about the business and treated it like their own.

This meant they had *connections* across all areas of the business. They knew who to talk to when there was a problem. They understood chain of command, but they had good relationships across the board. These relationships allowed them to bypass normal channels when necessary.

They didn't care who got the credit. They wanted to make FedEx a success.

You don't have to *be* an entrepreneur to *think* like an entrepreneur. Consuming information helps you begin to think like a shareholder. I'd been doing that for years at FedEx. But C-4 Leaders don't stop there. They take it one step further. They not only consume information, they develop a system for connecting the dots.

YOUR GOAL SHOULD DEFINE YOU, NOT YOUR POSITION

When starting a business, an entrepreneur often can't afford a marketer or a salesperson; they have to be able to do it all to reach their goal. They can't worry about their title or the work that needs doing won't get done. When I got to know the STP, I started thinking about how common it is for people to define themselves by their field of study. It got me to start thinking about the *why* behind that thinking.

My brother worked at McDonald's for twenty years. He started at age fifteen and worked his way up. When you hear that someone works at McDonald's, you probably think of a teenager with no experience working their first job. When you hear about an adult working at McDonald's, you may think that they don't have the drive to pursue a different career.

When I thought of my brother, I didn't think of him as the teenaged burger-flipper. In my mind, he was the thirty-year-old store manager. Same company, but vastly different jobs. Because my brother had started at the bottom, he'd done all the jobs. He'd cleaned the restrooms, emptied the trash, worked the cash register, been a shift supervisor, and eventually worked his way up to manager. By thinking like an entrepreneur, he showed that he could do it all, but he was smart enough to work into a position where he didn't have to.

My father started out as a janitor at St. Jude Children's Research Hospital. Although that was his job description, he actually owned his own janitorial service company. At St. Jude he never thought of himself as "just" a janitor. That may have been his title, but his ambitions were much higher. Now, forty years later, he's not only still at St. Jude, but he has achieved the position of Director of Environmental Services.

After getting to know the STP who got it done, I realized how much I'd slipped into that thinking of defining myself by my title and field of study. In the city of Memphis, FedEx employs over 40,000 people. Everyone is familiar with FedEx—especially with "the Hub," where packages are sorted and shipped. But I realized that whenever someone would learn that I worked at FedEx in Memphis, they would assume I worked in the Hub. I was quick to correct them and say, "Oh no, I work in IT."

I wasn't thinking like an entrepreneur. To my shame, I was actually looking down on the people working in the Hub, as if that job was somehow beneath me. After that night when the systems crashed, I changed my thinking. Shipping packages is what we—all of us at FedEx—do for a living. If I'm ashamed of that, then I've created my own ceiling and limited my growth potential.

From that point on, I redefined myself—not by my position, but by the goal.

Now when anyone asks, I tell them I ship packages for a living. The sign on my door says *Chris Winton, VP of HR*, but without those packages in the Hub, I wouldn't have a job. My dad's a janitor. My brother works at McDonald's. And I'm darn proud of both of them. Their goals, and the people they help when pursuing those goals, drive them to greatness regardless of title.

If you want to be a C-4 Leader, you can't let your title or your field of study hinder your trajectory. Forget about the piece of paper you got in school and see what your experience and determination can do to make you an asset to your company. Mine the lessons from both your successes and your failures. Look beyond the sign on your door to see where the problems are. You might just have the right blend of experience, determination, stubbornness, and curiosity to become an STP.

Defining your goal requires you to begin with the end in mind. Ironically, it was my daughter Jordyn, who was twelve years old at the time, who really drove this lesson home for me. When she was ten years old, she decided that she wanted to write a book. I'd see her working on it from time to time and was proud of her persistence. At her age, I couldn't even make it through reading a book, much less trying to write one of my own.

For two years, she plugged away at her book. She made good grades in school. She played soccer and basketball. Yet as busy as she was, she still made time to work on that book. Finally, I asked her what kept her going. Her response was brilliant. "Dad, I wrote the last chapter first so I knew how the story was going to end."

Huh. That sounded pretty smart to me.

Then she explained that she wrote the title of each chapter in reverse order. She said that gave her a jumping-off point for whenever she had time to write. She knew what the chapters needed to be about because she knew *how the story ended.*

My little girl taught me a lesson that I began to diligently apply to my own life. My daughter knew how to connect the dots of her story because she had mapped out the checkpoints along the way. She didn't care that she was just a kid in 6th grade.

In her mind, she was the author of a book. She didn't have an English degree and she didn't need one. She didn't have a book publisher; that was a later problem. She didn't have anything but a great story to tell and a desire to tell it to the world.

The next time I sat down with my leadership team, I challenged them with a new way to look at the next fiscal year. "Instead of writing our goals for the year, we're going to write our results." I had them think twelve months ahead and work backward from there.

They knew I wanted them to consume the right information, but this method of working backward from our desired results gave them the means to connect what they were consuming. Connecting the dots allowed them to take ownership of the process and more efficiently reach that destination.

CONNECT THE POSSIBILITIES

If you are feeling stuck and things just don't seem to be connecting, there are things you can do to break through and move forward. Everywhere around you are dots, pieces of information. These dots may be the people you work with, the tasks your team is responsible for, or the targets you hope to reach as an individual or a team. They can be lessons you are learning or challenges you don't yet know how to solve.

Most people don't, can't, or won't look for the connections between things. They stay in their silos, head down and focused on their little piece of the puzzle. They may be really good at their piece, but they'll never become a C-4 Leader.

C-4 Leaders connect the possibilities. They look at what is around them. They actively listen to what they hear. They learn to combine the lessons from their own life and the lessons they see lived out around them. When systems crash, planes are grounded, and mistakes are made, they don't freeze up.

"C-4 Leaders connect the possibilities."

Okay, maybe they freeze up for a moment as I did at first when our systems went down, but they are smart enough to take a step back, evaluate what they see, be willing to look for original solutions and then take decisive action.

If you want to learn to connect the possibilities in your life and leadership, then do these three things:

1. **DEFINE YOURSELF BY YOUR GOAL, NOT YOUR POSITION.**
   It doesn't matter where you are now—if you are reading this book, you likely have bigger aspirations and a desire to learn and grow. That's excellent! Learn all you can from your current position but don't let it limit you. Your position is the vehicle, your goal is the destination.

   Seek to become the best person you can be in that role and add value to those around you. Chances are, people are watching and will steer you in a direction you may have never thought of. That's largely how I ended up in HR from IT. I sought to add value to people wherever I was. Influential people who were higher up than me took notice. Your position is part of who you are, but it's not all of who you are. Don't let it limit your ability to look out and connect the dots.

2. **IDENTIFY YOUR SAME TEN PEOPLE.** Look around. Take a moment to think about who really gets things done in your department, division, or organization. They are the people who everyone knows, but they aren't showy or pushy. They just seem to be around when things need to happen. This isn't a coincidence. And in most cases, it's not self-serving. They genuinely want to help make the organization better because they are serving a cause that is bigger than themselves.

When you identify your STP, seek them out. Ask them to sit down for a cup of coffee or take them to lunch. Develop a list of genuine questions to ask. Get them talking about how they add value to the team and organization. Ask them about the lessons they've learned from their lives. Passion is contagious. See if you can catch some of theirs.

"You don't have to sit back and wait for things to happen; you can go out and make them happen."

3. **CONNECT YOUR POSSIBILITIES.** Everything in your business is connected. The people, the processes, the problems, the potential—everything is interdependent. The good news is that if you are in that web of connection, you have the potential to make a difference. This truth should be empowering! You don't have to sit back and wait for things to happen; you can go out and make them happen.

How can you connect what you know and who you know to get things done? You may be able to become one of someone else's STP. You may be able to bring an outside perspective to a situation by using the information you learned from a previous job or experience. Often a new way of thinking is crucial to get things unstuck. Develop possibility thinking by connecting to the larger vision of the organization.

For example, FedEx is a shipping company. We ship packages. From the CEO to the most recent hire, we are all dependent upon those packages rolling into our doors and out onto our trucks and planes. I'm proud of that.

If you want to shatter the self-imposed limits of your glass ceiling and become a C-4 Leader, you've got to learn to connect the dots around you. Think like an entrepreneur. Solve problems as if it was *your* business and *your* livelihood depended on it. You may just discover a solution that no one else has seen. You may become indispensable. You may find yourself with a seat at a table with new people and new possibilities.

When you connect the dots, you just never know what's around the corner.

CHAPTER 8

PEOPLE & POSSIBILITIES

PEOPLE GET UNCOMFORTABLE when you don't follow a traditional path.

It's not hard to see why. Most of us are conditioned to get on the path and stick to it. It's like one of those moving sidewalks in the airport. You may spend some time ramping up to match your speed with it's speed. Then you take your first step on the sidewalk and feel it moving under your feet. You steady yourself for a moment or two and then, *whoosh*, you're on your way.

Most people go to school, get a job, and get on "the path." It may be a path to rise through the ranks in your field, as I was doing in Information Technology. It may be to climb the ladder to the corner office on the executive level. It may be to simply be "the boss."

Whatever it is, one thing is true: you aren't the same person today as you were when you first walked through the door and took your job. You've grown, changed, experienced new things, and learned what you like and don't like.

But this is the point where most people get stuck. They stay so focused on the *path* they started on at the beginning of their career that they fail to look up and see the possibilities ahead of them.

What if the path you are on is not the right path? Then what?

DON'T PUT ME IN YOUR BOX

This was the question I found myself thinking about more and more when I was in IT. It's not that I was unhappy in IT, I was thriving there. I simply wanted to open my mind to other possibilities. That's what C-4 Leaders do. They constantly adjust their thinking to be sure they are connecting the dots and seeing both people and possibilities.

When I decided to leave IT and take a new path, some people thought I was crazy. I had a flourishing IT career where, way back when, I'd started as an intern and had been promoted all the way up to director.

As a director in IT, I was leading culture change. The Chief Information Officer knew who I was and kept me on his radar. When he asked me to take the stage at that all-management meeting for a few moments, I made even more of a name for myself. He seemed to like my performance with his quipp, "Note to self, don't follow Chris Winton."

After that, everybody knew that if the CIO likes Chris Winton, he's on the upward track. In IT, who is better to help you move up in your career than the actual Chief Information Officer?

So it came as a shock (to say the least) when I made the jump from IT to HR. There was a constant rumble of comments that came my way:

Wait a minute, Chris, you're going to HR? What are you doing? You've built the IT dream career. You've got the notoriety; you've got sponsorship from the CIO. There are more than 20 Vice President positions and more than 10 Senior Vice President positions in IT. You could easily get to that point in your career.

No one understood my thinking. People questioned why I would leave IT to go to HR. In Human Resources there are only two

Vice President positions and only one Chief HR officer. Everyone asked me, *Why would you limit yourself?*

I spent so much time and energy trying to answer that question that I finally got fed up and tired of answering and just started responding, "I don't owe you an answer to that question. I'm more than an IT guy. Stop putting me in your box. "

I was moving from what was *perceived* success, toward more personal *fulfillment*. I was excited by the possibilities I could see ahead as my purpose, passion, and profession came together. In IT, I felt limited by who I could influence and what I could accomplish. My path was changing, but a new path always brings new possibilities.

HAVE YOU EVER RECONSIDERED WHAT YOU DO?

Have you ever faced a decision like that? Maybe you've been put in a career box and you're desperately searching for a way out. It may be a prison of your own making. It can be incredibly frustrating to feel stuck. It can be even more frustrating when you are good at what you do but you don't hold the same passion for doing it as you once did. Then it almost seems irresponsible to take a jump.

Breaking out of the career box and pursuing something different takes incredible courage. In a real sense, career boxes can become self-imposed glass ceilings. It takes some high-powered explosives to break through. I was a rising star in IT. Technically, I had it made. I could stay on that moving sidewalk and let it take me all the way to a VP position and possibly beyond.

But doing so would have meant being dishonest with myself about who I was and the work I hoped to achieve. It would have been a nice way to make a living, but it wouldn't have made me happy with my life.

Stepping out of your box challenges the status quo. It's important to know that most people simply want you to go along and get along. They've identified you as something—IT professional, lawyer, janitor, salesperson, web designer—and they don't want you to change. It helps them make sense of their world to see you stay stuck in yours.

Most people start defining themselves by their profession. What they do becomes who they are. Over time, it becomes difficult to differentiate between the two. They think that one day, if they get lucky, they might get to align a little bit with their passions. But to change jobs to try and find that passion, well, that's just too great of a risk.

That's the question people were asking me. They could only see the things I was giving up. I could see all the possibilities that were coming my way. In that space was all the difference. I've seen and coached countless people who stayed stuck, just hoping something would come their way. That's no way to live.

Many times people won't make the right move because they fear the sunk cost. But it's a matter of perspective. If sunk cost is the driving factor, then you'll stay where you are. You'll figure you've spent this much time working in your career to this point and won't want to waste it. When people tell me this, I'm always surprised. I ask them, "But if you're unhappy, are you willing to be unhappy for the next twenty years, because you don't want to avoid the sunken costs?"

Most people choose a profession, but they never make sure that profession connects to their purpose and passion.

To my way of thinking, moving from unhappiness to happiness, from profession to purpose and passion is worth the potential risk. Most people choose a profession, but they never make sure that profession connects to their purpose and passion. These three rings are critical; get them to intersect and you've found your sweet spot.

When you're trying to define your goal, you need to factor all three in. Ask yourself this question: *What is my current path and is that the path I want to be on?* If you lead people, you need to ask them that question, too. It doesn't do you any good to keep a person in a role that's a poor fit for their skillset and passion. It's better to help them find a place where they can shine. That's what I get to do now in my HR role, and I find it incredibly rewarding.

It's never too late to begin with the end in mind. If you're in IT and think, "Well I'm *in* IT, so my goal must *be* IT." You aren't seeing the bigger possibilities. You have to recognize the pressures that may have contributed to put you there. Then you've got to break through them and think outside the career box. Maybe IT is where you are meant to be; maybe not. Only you can decide. But when you do, you've got to be prepared for the questions. Because they're coming.

A friend once told me about a person he coaches who is an emergency room physician. He hates his job. Can you imagine the sunk cost it took to become an ER physician? It must be staggering. But this guy wants to be a real estate investor. Now, he's got a decision to make. He's got to learn to listen in and determine if it's time to make the move. You can be sure people won't get it. To those closest to him, he's an ER doctor. That's quite an accomplishment. He fits nicely in that little box. If he makes the move, the label has to change.

Here's the point: Only *you* can define what success, happiness, or contentment looks like for you. You may have a good paying job. You may be climbing the ladder to success in your field. You may be in a position to make even more money. You may have increased prestige. That's all well and good, but C-4 Leaders don't get swayed by those things. C-4 Leaders have the courage to say "that's not it for me" and the wisdom to see *and pursue* other possibilities.

CONNECT WITH YOUR PURPOSE

Let me pause for a second and make something clear. It's important for you to hear what I'm *not* saying. I'm not saying that you should put this book down, storm into your boss's office, and slam a resignation letter on his or her desk.

First of all, that's just stupid. You're smarter than that.

"You'll never get on the right track unless you connect to your purpose."

Second, you may be in the right role. It may be a perfect fit for you. You may be leading people well and helping them succeed. If so, that's excellent. If you *are* feeling like you're in the wrong place, you've got to get clear on your purpose before you make a move. Otherwise, you're just taking those frustrations with you to the next job. If you don't address them, they'll follow you around for your whole career like a tail follows a kite.

You'll never get on the right track unless you connect to your purpose. It's as simple and complex as that. Everyone has a purpose; few people know what it is. Fewer still connect to it and use it to guide their lives.

You've already read some of my story. I started as an intern at FedEx and that led to a full-time job with them. I began making more money than I'd ever seen in my life. I bought my first house when I was twenty-one years old. I had the bachelor-pad white leather sofa. I bought a top-of-the-line Mitsubishi Montero Sport and parked it in the two-car garage. It was blacked out—man, was it nice! But why should I settle for four wheels when I could add two more? I bought a Honda CBR600 motorcycle, because what self-respecting twenty-one year old doesn't want a toy like that?

From the outside, I had it all. Inside, I felt emptier than ever.

I had achieved most of the goals I had set at INROADS with Alfonzo. I wasn't the CEO, but I was doing everything I had set out to do. I had all of the things I had been told made up the American dream. Yet I woke up one day and stood on my porch in Memphis, Tennessee in tears, trying to figure it out: *Why am I not happy? I've checked every box. What am I missing?*

It was the beginning of a radical change in thinking for me. At the time, I was engaged—we were getting married later that year—when a job opened up with FedEx in Atlanta. My new wife wanted to live in Atlanta, and I certainly needed a change of scenery. So I sold a bunch of my stuff and took I-22 South until it hit I-20 East. We hung a left and started our new adventure. I was on a search to figure out what I was here for and wasn't going to stop looking until I knew the answer.

The first clue came not long after we settled in Atlanta. Out of the blue, I got an email from a friend that I had known in college. She wrote:

> *I've been looking for you for the last three years just to say thank you. I wanted you to know that God put you in my life that day when we saw each other in the Fogelman Building at the University of Memphis. I had no idea what I was doing in school, and you talked to me about management information systems. You explained what that degree was and you started talking to me about certifications. I wanted you to know that I'm now a certified network engineer for the City of Millington, and I owe it all to you.*

I'll never forget the feeling I had when I read that note. It took faith for me to leave Memphis and move to a new city. It took faith for me to leave IT and move into HR. And it will take faith when I make the next leap, wherever that may be.

For the first time, I had a little hint of what I was made to do. I had been going through the book *The Purpose Driven Life* by Rick Warren. It was peppering me with thought-provoking questions. The email was confirmation that my whole life to this point had been about connecting dots and helping people reach their full potential. Steve Jobs once said, "You can only connect the dots looking backwards." It was true for me and with a sudden realization I could see that it had been there the whole time.

When you begin to connect the dots in your life, you see the possibilities for what could be. That's why making the jump from IT to HR was a no-brainer for me. The people who were questioning my decision (and even my sanity) had never seen that email. They'd never seen the process I'd been going through for over a decade.

For them, it looked like a hard left turn. For me, it was the next logical step.

It's interesting how the words you speak frame your mindset. I had always referred to myself as an IT guy. So I was incredibly thankful that the guy in compensation had said to me, "Man, somewhere in your life you zigged when you were supposed to zag; you're made for HR." HR had never even been on my radar. I certainly wasn't even thinking about a profession in HR. But when I stepped into this space, it was the most natural thing I've ever done in my life. Why?

The goal of HR is to hire people and give them opportunities. My job is to grow them to their future career path. I get to inspire and motivate the workforce. Now, I realize how fortunate I am to get paid to do that. And it's humbling.

"I COULD PUT THESE KIDS TO WORK TODAY!"

Without the people in your life, you really have nothing. It may sound dramatic, but the first thing we connect with are people. If I'm interviewing someone for a job at FedEx, they don't connect to the organization first, they connect with me. If you meet someone who seems like they could become a good friend, you connect on a personal level first. You like their personality and the way they make you feel before you ever worry about anything else. People have a way of deepening connections.

That's why C-4 Leaders not only see the possibilities, they connect their people to their possibilities. That's how I got so passionate about the education space. Shortly after joining the HR department, we began working with the Obama administration to increase the opportunities for young people to go into tech fields. I was at a coding boot camp with kids from an organization called First Robotics.

"That's why C-4 Leaders not only see the possibilities, they connect their people to their possibilities."

I stood watching in awe as they kids demonstrated what their robots could do. I listened as two young guys talked about their robot throwing a ball in a basket seven feet away. Not to be outdone, the other guy said, "Man, my robot can make a basket from ten feet away!"

In the competition, you had to be accurate to get it into a bucket. The secret to that accuracy was in the code. As the 10-foot-shot kid started tinkering on the 7-foot-shot kid's code, I couldn't understand a word they were saying. I was amazed, so I asked them their ages.

Fourteen and fifteen. They both attended inner city schools, came from single-parent homes, and were totally outside of the typical demographic where we would expect to find programmers.

As I walked away, I was thinking, *I could put those kids to work today!*

When I got back to the office, I scheduled a meeting with the CIO. I described what I had seen and the raw potential that was waiting to be developed in these kids. I presented a plan to connect these kids to something bigger. In my mind, we had kids with LeBron James talent that were ready now. But the way the job's descriptions were written, we couldn't even engage them until years later.

I put my C-4 Leader hat on and went to work so we could hire them right out of high school. We changed the job description so it no longer requires a degree. Now we hire them right out of high school and pay for their college. We grow *with* them.

The program is called Pathfinder. We go into high schools and help kids figure out the right path. We look at the skills they already have and determine how to map those skills to an actual career with an in-demand job.

The White House puts money on the table for grants for these coding boot camps. We put grants in local communities for the same thing. Kids can now attend the boot camp for free to obtain and refine those skills so they're ready to hit the workforce. Then we hire them when they graduate high school as software developers.

Guess what? Most of these kids are nailing it! They're running circles around some of the experienced developers. But what's most amazing are their stories. When we connect and learn their why, we hear how they grew up in a trailer. Many have single parents and have seen how challenging it can be to pay the bills. They want to be able to take care of their families. So they are passionate about what they get to do. I've had more than one kid tell me, "If coding gives me the ability to take care of my family, then I'm going to be the best darn coder you've got."

These kids have found their *why*. And I've connected the right people to their possibilities. It doesn't get much more rewarding than that.

How do you connect people with possibilities? You infuse their passion with their profession. You connect them to the big picture. You think like an entrepreneur. You fight the urge to put people (and yourself) in a box. You let people be who they are and discover who they are meant to become. Do this and the rest will take care of itself.

C-3: COMMUNICATE

CHAPTER 9

LEADERS LOVE STORIES

COREY WAS ON my help desk team. He was one of the technical leads. A sharp guy, he definitely knew his stuff, but he had one problem—he had a huge chip on his shoulder. He would come to me almost daily and complain about what *this* person or *that* person didn't do. He would constantly question why leadership (and by leadership, he meant me) made certain decisions.

With Corey, everything seemed to be a half-empty glass.

The easy thing for me to do would have been to get rid of Corey, but I saw potential in him. So one day, after a particularly vocal gripe session, I just asked him, "Man, why are you so bitter?"

He looked at me like he couldn't believe I would ask him such a question. He was quiet for a second, but then he started talking to me about what was going on in his mind. I discovered that outside of work, he was an accomplished playwright. He had won awards for his work. He often spent his weekends doing plays at local churches and traveling. That's where his passion was, but by working the help desk his profession and passion were totally separated. It was causing massive friction within.

I thought for a moment before replying, then said, "Let's see if we can connect your passion to your role now." He looked at me, intrigued. At the time, we had a problem in our department. Understandably, the help desk job is a pretty mundane job—every day is the same thing. You pick up the phone and listen to somebody gripe and complain. Thick skin is a prerequisite for survival.

When your job is answering the phone to hear complaints all day, it casts a long shadow. Morale was low. So I suggested, "I can't change the job because that *is* the job. But what if you could help me get people excited about what we do?" He nodded his head.

I explained that I had a town hall meeting coming up and asked him to pull something creative together for me to rally the troops and boost morale. I gave him total creative authority. He looked at me like he didn't believe what I was saying. For a creative guy this sounded too good to be true. I reiterated: *total creative authority.* Just make it fun and make me proud.

He perked up as he left my office with a new spring in his step. I could almost see the wheels turning about the possibilities.

What Corey delivered a few weeks later totally changed the vibe in the help desk culture. Morale shot through the roof. People felt like they were part of something important. They were something bigger than just listening to people complain. They were a team.

At the time, the X-Men movie had just come out, so Corey wrote a short script based on the "Help Desk X-Men" and put together a top-notch video. It started with one of the help desk team members walking in the front door and going straight to the coffee pot. He looked around for a moment and dumped some sort of white powder into the coffee.

As it dissolved instantly, he walked away.

Slowly people start walking into the breakroom to start the day. What do people do first thing in the morning? They get their caffeine fix. One by one, as people came in and grabbed their coffee, they began to transform. Gone were the beaten-down, frustrated, tired help-desk workers. In their place were help desk superheroes. The Fed X-Men.

The video showed one guy sitting down at his computer to take a call. As the person on the line starts talking, he begins typing with lightning speed. His fingers are a blur. He looks down at his fingers and up at the camera like he's thinking, "Do I have superpowers now?" One by one they all morph into a super version of themselves.

Some were younger, all were faster, each was better.

As the music rose and the video came to a close, Corey panned the camera out for a wide-angle shot of the group. Dramatically standing in front of their cubicles were the men and women of the help desk. Their arms are crossed powerfully in front of their chests in the shape of an X. *The Fed X-Men.*

They all shouted in unison, "WE ARE FEDEX!"

In the town hall meeting, people roared with excitement. They loved seeing the video and how it made everyone feel. Something changed that day because Corey connected his passion and purpose with his profession. All it took was my asking a few questions and connecting people to possibilities. It wasn't hard, it just took intentionality.

From that day forward, whenever somebody was on a call and got stuck, people would look at each other, give a *we got this* look cross their arms in an X. As they began to help each other out, you could see the joy they found in their work. Corey had changed the culture with the power of a story.

STORYTELLING SETS YOU APART AS A LEADER

What is it about stories that makes them so compelling? You've probably noticed that I love to tell stories. That's why I've weaved them throughout this book. *Showing* through stories illustrates and brings things to life in a way that simply *telling* a lesson never can.

Even now, when I see the people on that help desk team walking in the hall, we greet each other with the X. That project transformed Corey's attitude so much, that he later became the manager of that team. We did a feature story on him through our *I Am FedEx* campaign that presented him as a both playwright (passion) and a manager of the help desk (profession).

Corey's story is special to me because it's a perfect illustration of how leaders must communicate. Typical leaders view people like Corey as problems. His attitude stunk, morale was low, and he infected the whole group. But as a C-4 Leader, I viewed Corey differently. He was an influencer; I just needed to help him change his message to be one of positive influence. Using *his* powers of story, Corey brought the whole team together and morale took a 180-degree turn for the better.

Vision statements and mission statements may look good on a company website or hanging on a wall for visitors to see, but let's be honest—internally, few people ever remember them. But they will remember the story you tell *with* them. It's why Maya Angelou wrote, "At the end of the day people won't remember what you said or did, they will remember how you made them feel."

Great stories invoke a feeling.

Here's the leadership lesson: you must be intentional about the feeling you're trying to invoke with the people you lead. Then you can determine what story gets you to a place where you can connect the people to the possibilities.

I don't share Corey's story so you'll be impressed with me. I share it so you can learn to look for the same type of opportunities in the people you lead. There are people whom you influence who might just need a nudge in a new direction. As a leader, you get to give them that nudge. I simply saw a good person with high potential who felt stuck in a job that didn't excite him. So with that short conversation about what he enjoyed doing *outside* of work, I was able to connect the dots to a need I had (the town hall meeting) and communicate a vision that would empower him to put his natural strengths to work (telling a story through video).

IT'S NOT ABOUT YOU

We've already discussed the importance of consuming the right information. That's C-1. We followed up with connecting what you've learned with the people and opportunities in front of you. That's C-2. The next step C-3 is all about Communication. You need to take in information, connect the dots, then relay what you know and what you see, ideally through story.

When you are talking to someone, your body language communicates 70% of your message. The good news is you can learn to master your body language. You can watch how you stand, the way you make eye contact, how you hold your arms, whether you make fists, and how attentive your face looks when talking. All of these mechanics of speaking are important and can be mastered.

"What sets you apart as a leader who communicates well is the ability to tell compelling stories."

You can also work to master your vocabulary. You can learn better word choices and speak with authority as someone who knows the material backwards and forwards. You can develop an authoritative speaking voice that takes command of the room or stage. You can *make* people listen to you just by the sound of your voice. But that doesn't mean that you are communicating. You've probably zoned out in plenty of meetings where someone was talking but the room was lost.

Body language, word choice, and style are all components of your communication that can be learned and improved. But none of them will set you apart as a leader. What sets you apart as a leader who communicates well is the ability to tell compelling stories.

People remember stories because stories are sticky. When I first realized how powerful stories were, I knew I had work to do. For most of my life I had considered myself an introvert. Public speaking was my number-one fear. Number two was snakes. (I'm a much better public speaker, but I still don't like snakes. I'm not trying to overcome that one!)

However, I have become a much better public speaker. I was the person who said *I just can't get up in front of the room and talk*. It's much too frightening. Now when people tell me that, I have to push back. Here's the thing I learned: speaking to others is *not about you*. It feels like it's about you because you only know your limited perspective. You are concerned with what you say, how you sound, if you are making sense, and whether or not people think you look stupid.

If these are your primary concerns, you are never going to be an effective speaker. You may craft a message that you've memorized. It may sound good to a casual observer. You may not say "um" or "uh" or ramble. But if it's all about you, then your message will lack soul. It will fall short and won't connect. You are communicating *to* the crowd rather than *for* the crowd. You are worrying about how you look rather than how helpful you are.

When I realized the power of my words, and more specifically the power of the stories I could tell, I knew I had to get over myself and do a better job communicating. I had to learn to love talking to others in a way that was helpful to them. I realized that I had to get over *me* and become consumed with helping somebody else. I couldn't hide behind being an introvert any longer. If I wanted to become the kind of leader I knew I could be—a C-4 Leader—I was going to have to open my mouth and get to it.

Because growth only happens when you're challenged, I signed up for a Dale Carnegie class on public speaking. Every week, for twelve weeks, participants of the class were required to stand up in front of the group and talk for two minutes. The first time was hard. Two minutes may not sound like much, but for an introvert like me, they were an eternity.

"True communication only happens when you are true to yourself."

After the second or third week though, to my surprise, I began to get better. It still wasn't easy, but my focus was shifting. I begin to discover how to speak from my truth with authenticity. I wasn't trying to impress anyone. I was trying to communicate with them. True communication only happens when you are true to yourself.

The first talk I gave was about describing a defining moment in your life. I told the story of how my wife and I struggled for years to have kids and shared the overwhelming feeling of joy when my daughter was born. I'm not an emotional guy, especially in front of people, but even now (she's a teenager) I'm tearing up as I think about it. I'd never really talked about this in any great detail before, but for the first time, I realized the power my story had over the room.

When you are able to talk about those defining moments in your life, you realize that's what people connect to. Beneath the veneer of our skin color, gender, education, or experience we are all remarkably similar. The people you lead all have fears, hopes, dreams, and ambitions. Theirs may be different than yours, but people will relate when you share your story.

Over the course of those twelve weeks, I discovered how to be clear and concise when telling a story. For example, fiction authors know just how much to say and just how much to leave to the reader's imagination. The same components of storytelling are important when you communicate verbally. You've got to share the highs and lows, the feelings, the tension, and finally, bring people into the moment where your story evokes a feeling in them.

Not all of your life has been highs. There have been lows too. I understood how Corey was feeling because I'd been on the receiving end of those complaining phone calls. I'd stood on my front porch thinking, *Is this all there is?* I've felt the drudgery of life, so I was able to connect with Corey's feelings.

Leaders can fall victim to the trap of being too optimistic. Life can be hard. Business can be stressful. They don't call work *work* for nothing. C-4 Leaders recognize all these things and use truth in story to speak to their people. They know that stories work no matter the audience. And stories connect and stick over time. The best stories have a manner of vulnerability and uncertainty.

Now, you may not know the final chapter yet. But that's okay. Be honest with your people. When stories are done right, they can even become a part of your culture.

STORIES STICK

That Dale Carnegie course helped me to learn how to talk in story form. It instilled in me a desire to spend every day looking for stories. It's now become second nature to me because I've seen firsthand how powerful the leader who tells great stories is.

Not long after I finished my class, I became a certified trainer for Dale Carnegie. Now, the introvert who was anxious for his first class was the one leading classes. A guy in one of my classes, Steve, had a horrendous stutter. As you can imagine, at first these two minutes were incredibly difficult for Steve. For years, I had been taught that in speaking you have to be articulate. Don't say *uh*. Enunciate your words. Use proper grammar. Steve had none of these things on his side. I was at a loss for how to coach him.

His first couple speeches were brutal. And you could tell the class of about thirty people felt it, too. No one likes to be in a room where the speaker is struggling through a speech. It was painful.

But when we got to the session where people shared a low point in their life, everything changed for Steve. When I asked for volunteers, Steve was the first one to stand up. As he walked to the lectern in front of the room, you could almost hear the room gasp. He usually waited until almost the very end to speak.

Steve took a deep breath and started to talk about the point in his life when he began to stutter. The entire room was so quiet you could hear a pin drop as he began to share his story. One day, he was walking out of a grocery store when he saw a woman being robbed in the parking lot. His instincts kicked in. He ran to help but didn't notice the robber had a gun. As Steve's thudding footsteps alerted the robber, he turned and shot Steve one time. The bullet ripped through his throat and did severe damage to his vocal cords. Months later, after multiple surgeries, Steve was left with this horrendous stutter.

His powerful story transformed how we saw Steve. We were proud of him for rushing the attacker to help the woman. We were compassionate because the story showed us the kind of person he was. Everyone in those classes wanted to see their peers succeed, but Steve became special.

I always remember that story because during those two short minutes, I don't remember Steve stuttering one time. I didn't hear the stutter, I heard the story. He still stuttered, but his message was so powerful that none of us realized it.

Great stories help block out all of the things that may be wrong with a message and focus on what is right. The *uhs*, the improper grammar, even stuttering can disappear when you captivate your audience. They filter all of that out when your story grabs them.

When you're communicating—especially to large groups and teams—don't obsess about all of the stuff you've been told. Don't worry about how you look or exactly what you'll say. Don't give so much thought to what you are wearing. Don't worry about enunciating every word properly. All of that is superficial.

"The worst thing you could do as a leader is stand up without speaking truth."

The question you must answer is *what's the story I need to tell?* Let the truth speak. And if you don't know it, shut up. Because the worst thing you could do as a leader is stand up without speaking truth. People remember what you say when you make them feel something. C-4 Leaders communicate great stories in an authentic way. That's what sets them apart.

THE STORY THAT MAY NOT HAVE HAPPENED

Legend has it that, Fred Smith, founder and CEO of FedEx, wrote a paper when he was in college. According to the legend, his paper demonstrated the idea to one day starting a shipping company. Unlike its competitors, this future shipping company would span the globe. It would use a fleet of aircraft to send packages anywhere in the world. He envisioned a day where you could send a package almost anywhere literally overnight.

His professor was less than impressed and gave him a grade of *C* with the comment, "The concept is interesting and well-formed, but in order to earn better than a 'C', the idea must be feasible."[1]

Smith graduated from Yale University, enlisted in the United States Marine Corps, and served two tours of duty in Vietnam. When he came home, he still had the idea in mind to start FedEx.

That story has been floating around for fifty years. If you Google it, you can find articles written like the one that contains the quote above. It's part of FedEx lore. Over the last couple of years, as I've been speaking and developing the C-4 Leadership model, I'll often ask people in the room if they've heard about Fred Smith's term paper.

Nearly every hand in the room rockets up. Then I'll ask them if they know what grade he got on the paper. When I ask them to yell out the grade, everyone yells, *"C"* at the top of their lungs.

Once the noise dies down, I ask them a couple of questions: *How do you know? Have you talked to the chairman?* Then I let them in on a little secret that I've learned from my seat at the table. Fred Smith, the Founder, CEO, and Chairman of the company will neither confirm or deny that the story is true.

That is the power of storytelling.

Globally, 450,000 employees all know that their ultimate boss wrote a paper in the 1960s that predicted the creation of the company that signs their checks today. They know the professor was less than impressed. They know that he received a *C* on that paper.

In spite of never having met him or asking him the question, *they know.* That story has perpetuated because stories have power.

As a C-4 Leader, don't stand up and read a vision statement, because nobody will ever remember that. Turn your vision into a story. That's how you get everybody talking to each other, telling the story you want them to repeat. Stories stick. They communicate. Great leaders learn to love stories and use them to communicate their message.

CHAPTER 10

GET IN THE STORY ZONE—AND STAY THERE

HAVE YOU EVER been *in the zone*? You know, that place where everything is working for you and nothing can go wrong?

If you're a salesperson and you're *in the zone*, every call you make ends in a closed sale. If you're bowling *in the zone*, every frame is a strike. If you're driving to a meeting *in the zone*, every light is a green light. If you're at a party telling jokes *in the zone*, everyone is hanging on your every word and waiting for the punchline.

There's a funny scene in the movie *White Men Can't Jump* with Woody Harrelson and Wesley Snipes. Harrelson's character is Billy, a white former college basketball player who hustles players in pickup basketball games. Most of them believe he can't play just because he's white. Snipes' character—Sidney—is talented and cocky, and twice falls to Billy's skills on the court.

One of Billy's claims is that he can get *in the zone* where nothing can distract him. The on-court exchange between Billy and Sidney goes something like this:

"Give me the ball, man, I'm in the zone! When I'm in the zone, I can't miss!"

"Man, what is this zone you're talking about?"

"It's the zone, man. When I'm in the zone nothing can stop me! Just give me the ball."[2]

You don't have to be a ball player to know this feeling. When things are going your way, it can feel like you're unstoppable. But what is "the zone" and is it something you can really create? Perhaps it will help if I tell you a story of the first time I felt like Billy—*in the zone.*

IN THE STORY ZONE

In the last chapter, I shared how I went from attending a Dale Carnegie class to becoming a certified trainer. I took a pretty intense certification course called Effective Communications and Human Relations. The entire process took eighteen months to complete, almost like getting a degree. If you've done the work of getting an undergraduate or graduate degree, you know that the last few months can be grueling. Sometimes all you can do is try to keep your eye on the finish line and put one foot in front of the other.

During the final part of my certification process, I was at a pretty low point in my life. My mom had been diagnosed with cancer, and my 35-year-old brother had just suffered a stroke. So I had a lot on my mind. But I didn't want to miss my certification and waste the past year and a half. So I pushed on, grinding it out so I could gain my certification.

One of the final steps in the process was to lead a mock class. The instructor sat in the back of the room with the other students and watched as I facilitated a class. By this time, I was comfortable in front of the room. I knew how to capture an audience's attention and speak clearly and with authority. But I was beat. I felt down. I was just gritting my way through it with every class a chore.

So when the Master Trainer said, "All right, Winton, you're closing out today's class." I took a deep breath and sighed. As facilitator, I had to close out the class with an inspirational speech, but I was feeling anything but inspirational. I was as drained as I'd ever been.

"My head's not there right now," I told him. "I don't know if I can do it."

He looked at me and said something I'll never forget. "It's never about *you*. It's about *them*. Do it for them."

He was right.

It's not about me. It's about the people I lead. I knew that I had to press through in spite of how I was feeling. The theme of facilitating a Dale Carnegie course was that it's always about the participants. I was there to inspire them and guide them. I could do this.

So, not surprisingly, I dug deep into my vault of stories and asked, *What story do I need to tell?* What came to me was good old Billy from *White Men Can't Jump* and his enthusiasm about being *in the zone*.

As I made my way to the front of the room, I gathered my thoughts. I thought about the message I believed they needed to hear. I thought about the people in that room. I thought about my Master Trainer's challenge to make it about them and not me.

Then I started talking.

I began with a simple question: Have you ever caught yourself saying *if it ain't one thing, it's another?* Sometimes we all have that internal self-talk about how bad things are going in our lives. It goes like this: If it isn't the car breaking down, the refrigerator is out. Or the air conditioning just quit working. Somebody just rear-ended me at a red light. Somebody just got sick. My hours are getting cut at work. My marriage is rocky.

If it ain't one thing, it's another.

I had their attention now, so I decided to really throw them for a loop and bring in *White Men Can't Jump*. (Pro tip: when you're telling stories, it's good to keep people on their toes and unsure of what's coming next.) When I asked who had seen the movie, a handful of people raised their hands. For the rest of the room, I shared the basic summary and described the conversation Billy and Sidney had about being *in the zone.*

Then I got to the point. Is being *in the zone* even a reality? Can it really happen? I paused to let the suspense build.

- -

"The zone is not a place, the zone is an approach."

- -

When I started talking again my voice was quiet, but every eye was on me and I had their undivided attention. With unwavering authority I told them that the zone is not a place, the zone is an approach. You don't wake up one morning and decide to *go to* the zone. You wake up and decide to *be in* the zone. It's an attitude. It's a way of living. It's a desire to push through when you don't feel like it.

Then I shared exactly how I was feeling as I stood in front of them. My mom and brother were sick. Work was a challenge. I didn't really feel like being up in front of the room right now. But I was committed to being in the zone.

These events in life are going to hit you, I encouraged them, but do you have the foundational beliefs and understanding to say that when it hits, I'm staying in the zone? Do you know how to respond when life hits you with all it's got?

Every person in the room was leaning forward, hanging on every word, so I went on.

I started talking about some of the principles we'd all learned from Dale Carnegie over the past eighteen months. Don't criticize, condemn, or complain. Smile. Take a genuine interest in life. Become genuinely interested in other people. Each of these principles keep you in the zone and change your approach to life.

It may not sound like much here, but it was one of those moments where everybody in the room stood up and started cheering and clapping. I had never felt anything like it before.

Literally, in front of that room, with all that was going on in my life, I was in the zone. That was my first speech ever feeling like that. I honestly don't remember everything I said. I don't know how many times I said "uh" or "um." I can't tell you about my grammar or mechanics. I'm sure somewhere in the rulebook for public speaking, it says don't reference a movie called *White Men Can't Jump*.

I didn't care about any of that. That day pushed me out of my comfort zone and got me comfortable with being in front of a room with no notes or PowerPoint slides. I simply let the fullness of who I was come out for all to see. That was the practice field for me to answer the questions, *How do I relay who I am in the form of a story that sticks?* It was open, authentic, and real and showed me the power of story.

From the response of the room, I was in the story zone. And I wanted to stay there.

I SEE DEAD PEOPLE

The story zone is powerful. It's where lessons get learned and behavior gets changed. Communication through story cuts across all ages, races, genders, and socioeconomic levels, because stories are universal.

As an IT person who made the jump to HR, I have a unique way of looking at things. That's one of the ways C-4 Leaders learn to shine and shatter their glass ceiling. They understand the things that make them unique and, rather than run from them, run to them. They use them as a competitive advantage and for the good of the people they lead.

Those days when I began watching CNBC in the mornings as I got ready for work, I started to pick up on a potentially disturbing trend. I saw it because, as an IT guy, it spoke my language. But as an HR guy, I could see both the potential danger if we didn't get it right and the incredible opportunity if we did.

Every morning, I was consuming information that expanded my knowledge. I kept hearing that the labor market in the United States was heading for a STEM shortage. STEM is an acronym for *science, technology, engineering,* and *math.* The STEM acronym was first introduced by the U.S. National Science Foundation in 2001 with a goal to equip schools to help young people—especially women and minorities—focus on STEM careers. Since 2001, STEM-focused curriculum has expanded globally to schools around the world and become a major driver of the education system.

As you can imagine, FedEx is an organization that heavily relies on the STEM disciplines. Without technology, we can't function. Without engineering, our facilities don't work. We need a steady influx of workers who are talented in these areas. It's one of the reasons I was so excited to attract the kids who were talented developers right out of high school.

Using my IT brain and my HR brain equipped me to make that connection before other people did. We were about to fall off a labor force cliff. The unemployment rate was falling every day, which is a good thing, but when we reached full employment of STEM talent, it was going to be a problem. We'd have more jobs available than people to fill them.

As I started to connect the dots with what I was hearing on the news and what I was seeing in the marketplace, I had a chilling realization: we were about to go to war. But there was one problem. The internal leadership didn't see it as a war for talent. They thought we couldn't fill jobs because we didn't pay enough. They were looking at HR (me) and saying, *You just need to pay more.*

It's a common mistake to think that throwing money at a problem will make it go away, but that's rarely the case. I tried to explain that you don't solve unemployment with pay. That doesn't ensure you'll get the talent you need to do the job well. You can't buy your way out of unemployment; the labor market doesn't work that way.

I had to approach things differently. I had to get them to see that we're about to go to war for talent. And if we wanted to win that war, we needed a battle plan. But the people around the decision-making table are all people with extensive track records and big egos. So I couldn't just bring my suspicions that we were in a war for talent to the table without a good story. That's not how I work. It was time to open up the story vault again.

When I did, I came up with another movie. In this one, no white men had to jump. It's just a good old-fashioned mess-with-your-mind thriller. At the next CIO's staff meeting, with all his senior leaders present, I had a plan. I knew what I needed to do to catch their attention. I figured I'd go big or go home.

When they walked into the room, I had put an image up on the screen of Bruce Willis from the movie *The Sixth Sense.* It's a trippy movie where Willis' character, a child psychologist named Malcolm Crowe, tries to help a young boy named Cole Sear. The boy had an eerie ability to communicate with the dead, and the line *I see dead people* coming from the mouth of this innocent little boy became a chilling catchphrase.

When everyone was seated around the table, glancing up at the image on the screen, I let them sit in silence for a minute or two. When they started fidgeting in their seats, I walked to the front of the room and, in a quiet voice, said, "I see dead people."

That got their attention.

I looked at these men and women who I greatly respected and asked them if they'd seen the movie. They all indicated that they had. I told them, I'm the little boy in the movie who sees dead people. You are all Bruce Willis's character.

I started to get some puzzled looks.

"Do you remember what happened to Malcolme Crowe at the end of the movie?"

If you haven't seen the movie, I'm about to spoil it for you. All throughout the movie, Crowe is trying to help Cole deal with this issue of seeing dead people. As he's working with the boy, he's noticing that people are becoming more and more distant. This is especially true between Crowe and his wife. Although they live in the same house, they pass like ships in the night with hardly a word spoken between them.

Are you ready for the twist? At the end of the movie, Crowe finds out that he's actually one of the dead people. The whole time he's been helping Cole, he's been a dead man himself, but *didn't even know it.*[3]

So when I asked the room if they knew what happened to Bruce Willis's character in the movie, I had their attention. I clicked Bruce Willis off the screen and moved to my next slide where I walked through why we were approaching a war for talent. I had the facts and figures to back it up, but the only way I got them to listen was by capturing their attention with a story.

Slowly, heads began to nod around the table. Not because they were sleepy, but because the message was getting through. No one wanted to be the dead guy sitting around the table unaware that he's dead. We left the meeting unified that we had an issue and needed to work hard to solve it. It wasn't critical yet, but it would be if we didn't take action now.

At the next all-management team with our CIO, I was asked to speak about how to get the STEM talent we needed to continue to thrive in the marketplace. This time I brought a prop to go with my story. It was Malcolm Gladwell's book *David and Goliath*.

I held the book up and began talking about the story of David and Goliath. You don't have to be a person of faith to know the story. David was a shepherd boy who, although young and small, was strong and courageous. When a giant (nine feet tall according to the story) was taunting the army mercilessly, David took offense and decided to face the giant with just his sling and five stones.

If you hear a pastor tell the story, it sounds like David simply slung his rock in the general direction of Goliath, hit the giant in the head, and killed him. But that's not the case.

In Gladwell's book, he presents David as an *expert* slinger. When you read the story of David in the Bible, he was a warrior. He'd fought lions and won. He'd been practicing with his sling every day. He could hunt and kill with it. When it came time to fight the giant, he had five rocks—he was prepared for anything—but it took just one to kill the giant.

I told the people in the room, "We've got a giant to face too. It's a war for talent. If we ignore it, it won't go away. But if we face it now, with five rocks, we can defeat it and thrive."

David killed his giant with one rock, but I knew we'd need at least five. I outlined my "Five-Rock" strategy for solving the war for talent.

As I knew it would, the story stuck. From that day on, people talked about the War for Talent and the Five Rocks. Each of the five points of this strategy helped us combat the war for talent. When it came, we weren't surprised. Our rocks were our tools and we pulled out the one we needed when we needed it.

AUTHENTIC COMMUNICATION CONNECTS

That day was just one more reminder to me that C-4 Leaders use stories to communicate. That's one reason why they need to consume information. As you can see, I love watching movies. I enjoy listening to podcasts or audiobooks. Everything I consume goes in the hopper. I'm not sure when it will come out, but when I need it, it's always there.

Then they connect the dots. If I hadn't leaned into my understanding of both IT and HR, I'd never have picked up on the impending STEM shortage. Connecting the dots doesn't mean you're always on, churning through information like a server shifting through data. It simply means that you know the answers are out there somewhere. You allow your subconscious to chew on problems in the background. You let what you've consumed start clicking together. When the pieces start to come together, you move to the next step to communicate the results.

The most effective way to communicate is through story. Stories give you a common language to talk about anything and everything. And a common language accelerates understanding. If you've ever gone to a country where you don't speak the language and try to get information, you can understand how frustrating this can be.

Stories don't have to be complicated or complex. There are many out there for you to choose from. They can fit your unique style (I mean, come on. *White Men Can't Jump* and *The Sixth Sense?* I'll bet you didn't see those coming when you opened this chapter!)

C-4 Leaders learn to communicate with the people they lead. There is no confusion. There are no mixed messages. There's simply honest, authentic communication and trust. That's it.

It takes practice to get in the story zone, but once you are there and communicating effectively, you'll never want to leave. Your message will resonate with people around the table, and you'll be ready to take the next step.

C-4: COACH

CHAPTER 11

THE VITAL LINK

IT DOESN'T TAKE too many trips around the sun to figure out one very important lesson: life doesn't always go the way you planned.

When you're in school, sometimes your best work isn't enough and you don't get the grade you'd hoped for. That teenage romance you thought would last forever ends with your heart broken. The school you dreamed about doesn't offer you a scholarship and tuition is way more than you can afford. You graduate, but your job prospects aren't that exciting, so you go to work in a job that doesn't really light you up. You lose someone you love to an unexpected illness.

Life can have some unexpected turns, but not all of them are negative.

Sometimes, you surprise yourself; your hard work pays off and you get the good grade. Maybe your highschool sweetheart becomes the love of your life. You get married, have kids, and the love you have for each other grows as your family expands. Your backup school ends up being the best thing that could have happened to you, because it pushes you into a new place. You get a degree and create friendships for life. The job that didn't excite you has actually become incredibly meaningful, or maybe it led to a connection who led to another connection who led to a great job. Even death can shine a light on what is important and cause us to reorder our priorities to focus on things that matter.

Life is filled with highs and lows, ups and downs. It's a roller coaster of emotion. If you aren't careful, it can wear you out. You never know what the next day will bring, and that keeps you on your toes. Sometimes it can feel like you are trading punches with a heavyweight boxer. One minute you're throwing haymakers that connect with power, the next you're on the mat, looking up at the lights and wondering what hit you.

If you're lucky, you go through life with strong connections—these are the relationships that help you make it through the tough times and celebrate the great times. The truth is, we all link to one another in some way. Like an anchor on the end of a chain, we can drag each other down if we're not careful. We can also lift each other up when we are intentional about connection.

Here's what I've learned as I've coached and connected with people from all walks of life. We all have a "life-defining moments chart." It may not be on paper, but it's in our head at all times. It's a running list of the high points and low points of our life. It unintentionally guides us. It influences our decisions because, hopefully, we learn from when things have gone right or wrong. It colors the way we see the world and how we interact with others. As a leader, you've got to understand your own highs and lows so you can understand and empathize with the people you lead.

Here's an exercise for you to try. Grab a blank sheet of paper and a pen. Go ahead, I'll wait. Now turn it sideways and sketch a line in the middle of the page from left to right. This represents the timeline of your life. On the left is the day you were born. On the right is the day in the future when you will die.

With the paper in front of you, close your eyes for a minute and relax. With your eyes closed, rewind your life chronologically. Start at the earliest good or bad memory and unpack your life from there. For example, getting accepted into INROADs was my first dot. Maybe for you, taking that trip to Disney World when you were ten years old was pretty magical. It goes above the line. Draw a little dot there. Maybe winning the state championship in the 11th grade was pretty amazing. That gets an above-the-line dot, too.

Losing your grandmother to Alzheimer's when you were a freshman in college... man, that one really hurt. That dot goes way below the line. Your GPA took a huge hit that semester, too. Below the line. But then you met that special someone and you knew life would never be the same. Back above the line we go with another dot. Graduating is above the line. Breaking up for a while goes below the line.

You get the idea. When you sketch your life out like this, you get a very clear picture of all of the ups and downs that have shaped you. My hope for you is that there are more ups and fewer downs. And I really hope that the future is straight up as you learn to crash through the limitations that are holding you back.

Over the years, I've probably done this exercise with a couple hundred different people. What's always fascinated me is that everybody's dots trend up. I've never seen a downtrend. Now, they may be down for a moment, but if you look at the trend overall, it's always up and to the right.

Here's the point. C-4 Leaders *understand* their lives. They have done the hard work of examining their individual journeys. They have considered the impact these events have had on their lives and leadership. They know where they are and have a clear picture of where they are going.

But more than that, they are aware that *every single person* they lead has their own history of life-defining moments. And these moments continue to happen every single day. Inside your team is a complex web of ups and downs, highs and lows. And they are constantly shifting. The good thing about these moments is that they add richness and depth to the story.

When, as a leader, you can tap into the moments and see how your moments links to theirs, you begin to move into the final step of the C-4 framework: Coach. It's the vital link that allows you to connect to people and help them reach their full potential. And as a leader, it's one of the most rewarding things you can do.

LEARNING TO READ YOUR PEOPLE

When I'm facilitating workshops, especially with senior leaders, I often talk about the shocks of life. As a leader, these things happen to you occasionally because you are one person. But the more people you lead, the more they are happening every day to the people around you.

As a leader, I used to struggle when these things happened to someone on my team. If someone had a sudden death in their family, I never knew what to say. You've probably found yourself in this position. It's awkward. Death sucks, and that's about the gist of it. But while I may know the person on my team, I didn't know their grandmother or step-dad or friend from high school that passed away. So I couldn't really say anything to help out, even though I was sympathetic to how they were feeling.

But then I realized they didn't really need me to say anything. As their leader, they don't need my words of wisdom; they simply need me to understand that they are *going through something* right now. That's it. They just need me to be observant enough to recognize that there is more to their lives than what I see from eight to five.

The way to do that is to remember what you felt like during your low moments. When I was reeling from the news that my mom had cancer, my brother had a heart attack, and my Dale Carnegie facilitator asked me to give a speech to the class, I remember exactly how I felt. The first thought that popped into my mind was, *Nope, that ain't happening.* But when it became clear that it *was happening,* I had to dig deep to get it done.

So when I learn that a team member just received a diagnosis of cancer in the family, I remember how that felt when I got hit with the same news. Then I can relate and understand. Life challenges are equal opportunity. They hit us all. How do you walk with people during those moments? By remembering how you felt when you've been there.

That's where I usually challenge leaders to reflect. I once coached a leader who clearly separated her personal life from work. She was very sharp and great at her job, but also very stoic in front of her team. I remember as I sat down with her, I could sense her emotional detachment from the team. As we walked through her defining life moments together, she told me her low point was the recent death of her aunt. I asked her if she had told her team what had happened, and how it made her feel. She looked at me like I'd sprouted a third eye and said she *never* talks about it.

I encouraged her to open up to her team. She didn't need to go around crying her eyes out in front of them, but letting them see she's human wouldn't be such a bad thing. As a leader, you need to understand your own feelings, so when one of your team members is going through something, you can sense it and respond accordingly.

"If you aren't adept at reading your people, you'll fill in the blank with whatever you think is wrong."

As a leader, you've got to learn to develop an awareness around your team and how they operate. You've got to understand their nuances and idiosyncrasies. The best leaders learn to read their people. They understand not only what they *are* saying, but also what they are *not* saying.

People will keep showing up to work even when things outside of work are falling apart. They probably won't tell you what's wrong with words, but it will come across in their performance. If you aren't adept at reading your people, you'll fill in the blank with whatever *you* think is wrong. And sometimes your biases start to show. What you presume is wrong may be totally off the mark.

When you check your intuition and lead with your whole self, you begin to pick up on the subtleties of your team. C-4 Leaders balance their leadership with intuition and insight. Maybe you just sense that something isn't quite right with a team member today. He's quiet, and he's not typically this quiet. Her body language has shifted and things just seem... off.

If you know how to read your team, you notice those shifts and don't just go straight to performance. You figure something else must be going on, and so you check on him. You ask what's going on and then you *listen* to the answer. He or she may not say much, but that team member will know you are invested in him and how he's feeling. And that is how you start to really know your range as a coaching leader and bring your whole self into the leadership role.

THREE TYPES OF LEADERS

Leadership is an interesting word because almost everyone has their own definition of leadership. The people below are authors, ministers, civil rights activists, military leaders, diplomats, presidents, and businessmen. Notice how their ideas of leadership vary:

> ➤ *A leader is one who knows the way, goes the way, and shows the way.* —JOHN C. MAXWELL

> ➤ *A genuine leader is not a searcher for consensus but a molder of consensus.* —MARTIN LUTHER KING, JR.

➤ *Effective leadership is putting first things first. Effective management is discipline, carrying it out.* —STEPHEN COVEY

➤ *Leadership is solving problems. The day soldiers stop bringing you their problems is the day you have stopped leading them. They have either lost confidence that you can help or concluded you do not care. Either case is a failure of leadership.* —COLIN POWELL

➤ *I suppose leadership at one time meant muscles; but today it means getting along with people.* —MAHATMA GANDHI

➤ *A leader is a dealer in hope.* —NAPOLEON BONAPARTE

➤ *Leadership to me means duty, honor, country. It means character, and it means listening from time to time.* —GEORGE W. BUSH

➤ *The task of the leader is to get his people from where they are to where they have not been.* —HENRY KISSINGER

➤ *Leadership consists of picking good men and helping them do their best.* —CHESTER W. NIMITZ

➤ *I think the currency of leadership is transparency. You've got to be truthful. I don't think you should be vulnerable every day, but there are moments where you've got to share your soul and conscience with people and show them who you are, and not be afraid of it.* —HOWARD SCHULTZ

➤ *Leadership is not about you; it's about investing in the growth of others.* —KEN BLANCHARD

All of their takes on leadership are different. If you want to shatter your glass ceiling and move up the leadership ladder, you have to develop your own definition of leadership. Your definition will come from your life experiences, the culture of your organization, the way you view yourself as a leader, and the impact you hope to have. For example, a military leader has different objectives than a business person. The business person has different objectives than a minister or non-profit leader.

But perhaps even more important than your definition of leadership is understanding the type of leader you are now, so you can see a clear picture of the leader you want to be.

There are three types of leaders. The first type really isn't a leader at all. Not everyone is cut out for leadership. Let's just go ahead and own it—not everybody is supposed to be a leader. Some people love to be in the background. Not everyone wants to be in the spotlight. If that's you, it's important that you recognize that. It doesn't mean that the C-4 Leadership message is wasted, it just means you apply the principles to your own career path. You still have to decide where you want to succeed. You still have to shape your charge so it clears out obstacles. You still have to commit to getting better. All of these things will help you shatter your glass ceiling.

The second type is the leader who can manage objectives, tasks, and get things done. That's really the majority of leaders. They know the target, motivate their people (sometimes in a healthy way, sometimes in an unhealthy way), and get things done. These are the managers. They manage their area of responsibility, but little else. They rarely reach out to other areas in their organization, because it's not their job. They don't tend to think like a stakeholder or an entrepreneur. They do their job—most of the time exceptionally well—but they look *down and in* instead of *up and out*.

The third type of leader, however, is much different from the first two. This is the leader that's in short supply, because they have the capacity to transform teams, departments, and entire organizations. These leaders are the ones who can see beyond the goal to the ultimate vision. They crystallize it as a picture in their mind and then use that picture to motivate, influence, and inspire everyone around them to go after it with everything they got.

They are coaches in the best sense of the word. They have a game plan and push everyone to be their best and perform at a world-class level. They know the strengths and weaknesses of each of their players and position them to win. They aren't grinders who wear people down. They are builders who lift people up.

That's the kind of leader in short supply. That's the leader who explodes to the top because they know a secret: *it's not about them.* It's about lifting others to greatness. It's about having one hand up *and* one hand down. It's about mentoring the people who walk through the door, hungry and eager to grow. It's about speaking truth and showing compassion. It's about making tough choices and following through. It's about consuming the right information, connecting the dots, and communicating with clarity, so you can coach with authority.

Those leaders are on the fast track to success. And they're bringing a trainload of people with them.

WHAT IS A C-4 COACH?

This last type of leader is really the heart of the C-4 Leadership Approach. This leader has put it all together. The beauty of this leader is that he or she can come in all shapes and sizes. You don't have to be at the end of your career to become this type of leader. You don't have to have years invested in your organization. You don't need fancy degrees or certifications. You just need a willingness to impact others.

Here are some of the attributes I've seen in some of the best coaches/mentors:

➤ **THEY STAY COMMITTED TO THE PERSONAL GROWTH OF THEIR TEAM.** In sports, a coach helps the individuals form a cohesive team with one goal—to win the game. Under that goal may be individual objectives, like getting better at your position, improving your batting average, or improving your free throw shooting. A coach can see things that the players can't always see and stays committed to helping each player improve. They work to establish goals and objectives with the team member and then create actions and milestones to help them accomplish them.

➤ **THEY CONTRIBUTE TO A POSITIVE SPIRIT.** Coaches create a shared culture and positive spirit. They create clarity around the future vision and help their team members see what is possible. They are honest about where to improve, but they never get down about whether that improvement is going to happen. Team members never leave an interaction feeling beat up or criticized; any criticism is constructive and leaves the team member energized and encouraged.

➤ **THEY HOLD PEOPLE ACCOUNTABLE FOR THEIR ACTIONS AND GOALS.** Coaches don't shy away from the truth. When they see something wrong, they speak up. When they identify an area of improvement, they tell the team member. They know and understand each team member's goals and keep one eye on performance and one eye on improvement. They know that the big picture is to produce a win, and that only happens with hard work, discipline, and determination.

> **THEY PROVIDE A VITAL LINK IN THE CHAIN.** In sports, people often talk about a coaching tree. For example, Nick Saban, coach of the Alabama Crimson Tide football team has former assistant coaches sprinkled all over the college football landscape. Each is linked to Saban and, in many cases, has maintained that connection. C-4 Leaders coach their team members by building bridges to others inside and outside the organization. Simply put, they know people their people should know and leverage those connections to help their people grow.

"The best coaches are available."

> **THEY ARE AVAILABLE.** The best coaches are available. They don't just say they have an open-door policy, they keep the door open. Through the highs and lows of life, they are there for their people. They become a sounding board and a voice of counsel. Good coaches don't monopolize their wisdom. They don't hold it hostage or use it to cement their power. They give it freely to people with high-potential; people who are likely to become coaches themselves.

Coaching is a vital link in the chain of growth. Just as a chain is only as strong as its weakest link, you are only as strong as the people you connect with and invest in. I've formed some of my deepest relationships as a coach. I've been on the receiving end of some things that were tough to hear, but they helped me change my thinking, actions, and, ultimately, my trajectory. Sometimes I've struggled to know what to do when *my* coach gave me a new way to look at an old problem.

Coaching is a mindset that separates the leader who simply gets the job done from the leader who empowers others to be better. It's become one of my favorite things to do. It all started because of a man who reminded me of the shadow I cast as a leader. The way I pay him back is by coaching others forward.

"Good coaches don't monopolize their wisdom."

CHAPTER 12

THE JOURNEY IS THE REWARD

JUST THE OTHER day I got to coach a group of individuals in a very special way. I call these groups Coaching Circles. I host them once a month in a small room on our corporate campus. These circles are limited to twenty people—I want it to be intimate enough where I can engage directly with the people in the room. I want them to feel like they are a part of something that is unique and special.

I've been holding these Coaching Circles for the last two years because there just wasn't enough time to meet one on one with the number of people wanting one-on-one coaching time with me. That's the benefit of connecting and coaching others, it just continues to grow. In this room, just like the name implies, we all sit in a circle. There are no tables and few distractions. My aim is to encourage real conversations about what it takes to break through to the next level.

It never ceases to amaze me how powerful these circles can be. I'm just a small part of it, but I work hard to make it incredibly beneficial to the participants.

Over the past two years I've seen both new and familiar faces. Some folks attend once while others, I'm convinced, may never leave. I open with a little disclaimer: "These are the thoughts and opinions of Chris Winton. These are not the thoughts and opinions of HR, these are not the thoughts and opinions of FedEx."

I'm only half joking when I say this, because I want them to understand that in that room, I'm Chris Winton. Sure, I'm the VP of HR. That's obvious. But I want them to understand that I'm more than that. I want them to understand that I will be brave enough to give them the candid insights they are really looking for, if they are brave enough to ask the right kinds of questions of themselves.

That's what a coach does.

He or she empowers people to act and take control of their situation. So in the room, I give them permission to ask me whatever they want to ask. I'm willing to put myself out there, because I genuinely want to help people break through that glass ceiling. Typically, these sessions become about people that have aspirations in their career.

"We're striving and working to become our best, so we can deliver our best."

Many times people come to me because they've set a goal and now they've met some resistance. They applied for the job, but they're not getting the call back, or even worse, they get the "Dear John" letter. This is something I can understand and speak to because I received a stack of them when I was trying to secure my first director-level position. So we talk through those issues they are facing. I share the things that helped me break through when I hit those same roadblocks. The obstacles to breaking through are surprisingly similar for every person.

In this small room, we sit around in a circle and simply talk. There's no big PowerPoint presentation. There's no executive conference table to separate me from them. We're just folks in Memphis, working for FedEx, shipping packages to people around the world.

We each have hopes and dreams, career aspirations and personal goals. We've had ups and downs in our lives, but we're not finished yet. We're striving and working to become our best, so we can deliver our best.

A NEW COACHING MODEL

For years, when I started out as an intern and worked my way up, I used to notice the way executives were introduced to a room or from the stage. There would always be a common theme, like, *She's the leader of this or that…* Or *He's been listed in the Top 40 under 40,* or the *Top 50 under 50.*

When I was younger, it really impressed me, but it also stressed me out. I was just Chris Winton, intern. Or Chris Winton, Help Desk Advisor. There wasn't a lot to add after my name to make me sound impressive. I started thinking, *Man, I've got to get some accolades if anyone is going to listen to me.*

I started spending my career trying to get degrees and accolades so that when someone saw my file, they would be impressed. Now, I realize how unimportant that all is. In fact, I ask people *not* to read my bio when they are introducing me. What I started to realize is this: your bio never tells the full story. It does a great job glossing over all of the highlights, but it misses one thing. It never talks about the lowlights you had to overcome to get where you are today.

It's one of the main reasons I set up the Coaching Circle. I wanted a place to *get real* and talk about the whole story. The highlights give the false impression that you need to check a bunch of boxes before you have the authority to speak into someone else's life and situation. Nothing could be further from the truth.

Every executive, at every level, has a list of lowlights that drove the highlights. No one has a certificate on the wall for the time they lost the company millions of dollars because the planes were grounded, but you can be sure it's something they never forget.

Good coaches own up to the low points, too. They share when things *didn't* go as planned. They share where their perfect plans blew up. But they don't stop there. They share what they learned and how it has helped them become a better leader.

Even though I'm still only in my early 40s, I've been mentoring people for the better part of fifteen or twenty years. It's important to understand that you *always* have something to give another person. Sometimes it's a word of wisdom, sometimes it's a listening ear, sometimes it's an example of how you failed but owned up to your mistakes. There's always something one person can teach another.

In those early days, a one-on-one mentoring approach worked fine because nobody really knew me. I liked people so I just mentored those around me in close proximity. I had all the time in the world and became known as *someone who cared*.

As I became more successful and started to move up the ranks, that list grew. I wanted to stay available, but there's only so many hours in the day. Because my schedule during the week got so busy, I made a commitment to come in early. If you really wanted to talk to me, I'd meet you in my office at 7:00 A.M. That approach worked for a while, but then those early windows started to fill up, too.

So I began mentoring people between 4:00 P.M. and 6:00 P.M until finally, I was out of hours in the day. Still, people kept coming. I realized I was on to something that was working. People were listening to me and something I was saying (I hadn't yet refined the C-4 Leadership Approach) was working. I was serving a need, but the model was not scalable.

I thought that maybe instead of mentoring people one-to-one, I should try a one-to-many approach. I looked for opportunities to put my Dale Carnegie training to work and speak from a stage. I found I could deliver a good message that resonated with the room, but I missed the one-on-one interaction that I'd get with individuals. I could inspire a room, but I couldn't really coach them. There was no way to address their questions in a way that was meaningful and deliver more than a quick burst or a shot in the arm.

If you've picked up on anything you've read in this book, I hope it's this: *I'm only here because of the people that reached down and pulled me up.* All along my career I've had people speak to me with authority and conviction. You've heard the names, Alfonzo Alexander, Larry Netter, Reggie Shaw (who I'm about to introduce you to), and others. They've coached me, cheered me, trained me, encouraged me, advised me, and even kicked my butt along the way when needed.

I wanted to be able to do the same for the people I coached.

That's when I started to realize I was telling the same stories over and over—whether to a crowd of hundreds or to an individual sitting across from me in my office. Why? Because C-4 Leaders get into the story zone and stay there. They know that stories are sticky and they facilitate communication. So I thought, *What if we could just get together in small groups and have these conversations?* I'd leave Chris Winton, VP of HR at the door and just be Chris Winton, the battle-tested leader who wants to give you the C-4 to help you shatter your glass ceiling and explode to the next level.

Not surprisingly, it's become a new and better way of coaching and leadership. I've found that in these small group sessions, with twenty people sitting in a circle or conferencing on the phone, we can quickly get to the heart of their issues. Most people have the same questions, because most people face the same issues. If I could tear down the barriers and get them talking, we could make some headway.

To say it's worked would be an understatement. It's impacted everyone in the room—perhaps me most of all.

WHO IS THE LAST PERSON YOU PULLED UP?

If you truly want to shatter your glass ceiling and reach your full potential, this is the last step—*you must pull other people up with you.* It's the only way to reach the top and be happy with yourself once you get there.

Remember the painting that Alfonzo from INROADS showed me when I said I wanted to be a C-E-O? It was called *He Ain't Heavy* by Gilbert Young. That painting made such an impression on me—and has shaped my view of leadership—that a copy now hangs on the wall in my office. Alfonzo told me then, "If you ever want to be a leader, you should be both hands at all times. The posture of leadership is this: One hand always reaching up. One hand always reaching down."

Here's my question for you: who is the last person *you* pulled up? You probably didn't make it this far in the book if you don't have one hand on the ladder pulling yourself upward. Unambitious people don't read books like this, because they aren't trying to get anywhere. I know enough about you to know you've probably already got one hand securely on the next rung.

But the other hand should be pulling someone along with you. It should be reaching out to coach others and lead them from the lessons you've learned on your climb to the top. It's easy to forget because climbing is hard work. It's easy to use both hands to keep climbing the ladder.

That's why that picture hangs in my office today. I don't ever want to feel like I've arrived. I've still got work to do and people to help. So do you. Keep pulling up, but take others with you.

One of the benefits of the Coaching Circle is it levels the playing field in a way. The format puts people in a room and allows them to just talk. It's informal, but invaluable. It brings out comments like this one someone made to me:

When I think of you, I think of you as the epitome of a servant leader. In your position, what is it in you that keeps you so humble? Because if I were you, I'd probably be a little cocky. So what is inside of you that keeps you humble, knowing what you bring to the table and knowing what you have to offer, but still lets you communicate with anybody on any level?

To answer that question, I need to tell you about a man named Reggie who pulled me up and set twenty-something year old me on a different path.

LEADERS LEARN TO SERVE

In my 20s, I was a handful.

I had the goods and I knew it. In my INROADS suit and tie, I looked sharp. From my internship, I knew the ins and outs of FedEx and believed I had an edge over the people just starting from scratch. My MIS degree was cutting-edge.

I had two hands on the next rung of the ladder and was ready to ascend to the top. I was a tech in the Hub, working nights, but I wasn't going to be there long. I knew I had leadership in my DNA. I was going places. I could feel it.

My director at the time was a man named Reggie Shaw. When I first started, Reggie said he had an open-door policy. He told his team that anyone could come see him at any time, we simply had to walk through the door.

So I decided to take him up on that.

I talked to his secretary and got an appointment on his calendar a couple days later. This gave me time to puff my chest up and think about how good I was. I saw my potential and was pretty sure Reggie would, too. So I strutted around my apartment and worked up my already-large ego to be ready to go when it was time to talk to Reggie.

Sure enough, his door was open as I boldly walked my big head through the door.

Reggie looked up at me, and with a raspy voice like the God-father of the Tech Support, he said, "How can I help you?" *Cue the Italian music.*

I knew exactly what I wanted. Remember, this was only a few years past my INROADS journal and my desire to be CEO. To be CEO, I was going to have to become a leader, and in my mind, the quickest way to leadership was to take Reggie's job.

I plopped down in the seat across from his desk and said, "I want your job, tell me how to get it." *For the record, this is not a good way to make friends with your boss.*

He paused and looked at me, poker-faced, "You think you can do my job?"

Unfounded confidence wasn't an issue for me, so I said, "Yeah, it doesn't look that hard." *Ah, to be twenty-two years old and full of that combustible mix of ignorance and unfounded confidence…*

The fake leather of his chair creaked as he straightened up and leaned on his elbows across his desk. I had his attention now. *That stick of dynamite I just threw was going to shake things up. I could feel it.*

Unfortunately, it exploded, but not like I had planned. And I was the collateral damage.

For the next thirty minutes, Reggie went on to chew me out. He blasted me up one side and down the other. He reminded me of who I was and what my actual job entailed. Then he ended with these words, which I've never forgotten: "Get your butt back out there in that Hub. When you get somebody to follow you, then come talk to me about leadership. You can't handle my job."

I was stunned, but I wasn't giving up that easy, so I told him, "I'm going to be back." And I kept my word. For the next *ten years*, we met every month. Reggie became one of those people who was really pivotal in my career. But it took him slapping me around and saying, "You ain't all that. Get that *S* off your chest."

I had to hear that a number of times for it to finally sink in. A few years later, I'd gone back to school, earned my Master's Degree, and applied for my first manager's position. I didn't get the job, but got a nice "Dear John" letter instead. I read the letter and thought, *That's okay. It was the first one. They already knew who they wanted. I'll just get the next one.*

So I applied for the second job… and got my second "Dear John" letter. I figured it must be politics or something. I just wasn't in the right circle. So I applied for the third job. And got another "Dear John" letter. Now, I was starting to get mad.

The truth is, in my immaturity, I was still making it about me. I fell into a little bit of victim-thinking. I thought, *Oh, no. It's the good ol' boys club. I'm not getting these jobs because I'm black.* By the fourth "Dear John" letter, I had added a new offense and even created a new classification—double minority. I was convinced I wasn't getting the job because I was black *and* young.

I'd worked up a good case of righteous indignation, so I called Reggie and said, "We need to talk. I'm being held back because I'm young and black." I could hear the silence on the other end of the phone. Reggie, (who, by the way, is also black) said, "Have you ever thought it might just be you?" (Remember, coaches tell the truth, y'all!)

Almost before he finished the question, I started listing my degrees, my qualifications, my certifications. He let me go on for a minute or two, before responding.

In his quiet, Godfather voice, he said, "Remember what I told you the first time you walked into my office? Is anybody following you? There's a difference between leading and managing. Leadership doesn't need a title or qualifications or degrees or certifications."

Then he hit me right between the eyes: "Tell me, how many people are following you? If I go around and asked your peers what kind of leader Chris is, what are they going to say?"

I was still not getting it. I said, "Well, give me the title, and I'll show you."

"Nah, son. You've got to *earn* leadership," he said. "When you earn leadership and demonstrate that people will follow you, you'll get the title." If I'm honest with you now, I hung up the phone feeling let down. It didn't seem like my mentor and coach was on my side. It was a lonely place to be, but it was exactly what I needed to hear.

I applied for (and didn't get) my fifth manager's job, when the message finally started to sink in. There was something I was missing. I was unwilling to keep banging my head against the wall, so I reached out to the director who didn't offer me the job to see if I could get some feedback.

When we started to talk, she shared some of the same things Reggie had shared with me, but for whatever reason, this time it clicked. I knew that if I wanted to become a leader, I was going to have to learn to take one hand off the ladder I was climbing and use it to pull others up. It was going to put me in a vulnerable position, but I was willing to do what it took to grow up.

PAY IT FORWARD

I didn't get a sixth "Dear John" letter. I got something better—a manager's job that no one else wanted. I became the Manager of the Repair Center in an un-air-conditioned warehouse near the airport.

It was hot and noisy. I managed a team of temporary contractors working for me. It was far different from what I had envisioned for myself as a manager, but it was exactly what I needed at the time to help me grow up.

When people see me now, they see the version of me that serves others well and helps people shatter their glass ceiling. But that only happened because I listened to Reggie and my other coaches and started applying what they said to my life. With this Manager position, I was about to come full circle and see what Reggie must have felt on that day I walked into his office and demanded his job.

"Your career is like a GPS. You've got to set the destination first."

One day, a young man named Kevin worked for me in the warehouse. On a hot summer day, Kevin walked into my office. His t-shirt was soaked with sweat. His old jeans were worn and dirty. He seemed to melt into the chair across from my desk, drained from the Memphis heat. But his voice was strong as he said, "Hey, man. I want your job. How do I get your job and get out of that warehouse?"

Wait a minute, where have I heard this before?

I couldn't help but flash back to that day in Reggie's office. Different kid, same message. But the lessons I'd learned that day helped me get to this place, and I wanted my leadership to be about serving others. I wanted to help Kevin do the same. As we began talking, I walked him through what he needed to do to move out of the warehouse and into a leadership position.

I started by telling him that your career is like a GPS. You've got to set the destination first. It doesn't matter where you are now; a

GPS will plot a path to the destination. His first step was to pursue his degree. I told him that if his goal really was *this* job, that was step one. We talked a bit more until he went back into the heat to finish out his day.

A couple of years later, Kevin came back to me and said, "Chris, I finished that degree. Will you hire me now?" I did. I hired him at the repair center. After I moved positions and became Director of the Help Desk, Kevin called me again. He said, "Hey Chris, I've got some technical skills. I want to come over and work on the help desk with you."

I knew what he was capable of, so he came over, and took a third shift position on the help desk. Next, I moved over as Director of the IT Command Center and IT Ops. Not long after the move, Kevin called me up and said, "I can do that job, too." I brought him over to work the second shift in IT Operations.

Today, Kevin is the Manager at the repair center. He's got my old job, the one he told me he wanted ten years ago. Oddly enough, his path mirrored my own journey. But perhaps it's not really that strange after all. When I first got promoted to director in IT by Larry Netter, guess whose office I was given?

Reggie Shaw's. The same one I'd first met him in all those years ago.

You start to realize a pattern when you live out the message of *He Ain't Heavy*. When you've got one hand reaching up and the other one reaching down, it's amazing the things that start to line up that you didn't even know were possibilities.

When it comes to coaching others, your intent matters. I helped Kevin because Reggie helped me. Coaches seldom get the glory. In fact, there are many times they help others and no one ever knows. Reggie didn't have to help me mature and grow. He did it because he cared about me. I'd like to think he saw something in me worth investing in. I did the same for Kevin because I saw his potential and wanted to walk alongside him in his growth.

In coaching, the journey is the reward. And the reward is one that keeps giving for years to come.

CHAPTER 13

IF I ONLY KNEW THEN, WHAT I KNOW NOW

IF YOU'VE MADE it this far in the book, you know a lot about me. Maybe more than you even *wanted* to know.

But I know something about you, too. Are you ready for it?

Here it is: *you are more than just your work.*

Every one of us is made for more. We want to be our best at work, no doubt. But no one just plugs in at 8 A.M. and unplugs at 5 P.M. You have a life outside of work and I'd venture to guess that the hours between 5 P.M. and 8 A.M. are where you *really* start living.

Here's something else I know. Too many people get things out of balance in their lives and end up miserable. They pour all of their attention in one direction and, for a while, become very successful in that area. But like riding a unicycle, you can only go so far out of balance before you fall over and smack the ground face first. It's not pretty, yet it's a danger I've seen happen time and time again with the people I've worked with. I saw it again when I started coaching.

In air navigation there's something called the *1-in-60 rule*. I'm simplifying it here to make a point, but basically it states that if you are flying one degree off course, then for every sixty miles you fly, you are a mile off track. After sixty miles, it's not too hard to course-correct and get that mile back, but imagine what that one degree could do on a flight of hundreds or thousands of miles.

It leads to a drastically different destination than the one you planned. And once you get there, you might not have a runway to land on. If you've ever flown on a plane, you know that it's hard to tell where you are going—especially if you're flying in cloudy weather. You have to simply trust that the pilot is paying attention to his instruments and keeping the flight on track.

But in your life, *you* are the one in control. You are the pilot. If you don't have a clear destination in mind and a plan to get there, you can quickly find yourself far away from where you wanted to be.

A PLAN FOR YOUR LIFE

When my wife and I were first married, we faced what many newlyweds in their twenties face: figuring out how to operate as one. If you remember earlier in my story, I was pretty cocky in my twenties. Let's just say that attitude didn't mix well with marriage. My wife was pretty quick to call me on it. Like most people who are young and in love, we talked a lot about our goals while we were dating. I wanted to be a millionaire and Coleshia wanted kids more than anything.

So almost twenty years ago, Coleshia and I sat together to write what we called the Winton Household Plan. We outlined a shared vision for our lives.

It began with a mission statement: *Our goal is to obtain the manifestation of "Total Prosperity" in all aspects of life, emphasizing the areas of faith, family, finances, career, and community.*

Then we set weekly, monthly, and yearly goals and objectives. It was comprehensive to say the least. We still have annual budget planning meetings. After twenty years, Coleshia has finally warmed up to that idea.

It was an ambitious undertaking for two people in their early twenties! But we knew that if we wanted to cash in *later*, we needed to do the hard work of planning *now*. What was unique at the time was that we were struggling. We set a goal to become millionaires, but we were beyond broke at the time, buried in student loan debt and all the costs of just starting out.

We also had been told we couldn't have kids, but having kids was a big part of our dreams for the future. I remember waking up at 2 A.M. and hearing Coleshia crying in the bathroom after a second doctor told her she likely would not be able to bear a child.

The twenty year-old me didn't know how to handle this, but I remembered what Reggie told me after receiving those "Dear John" letters—you first have to be a leader at home. So Coleshia and I established this as a daily confession: *We claim total debt freedom, flawless pregnancy/childbirth, and millionaire status today in Jesus' name.*

We committed ourselves to consuming any and all information related to these areas. From studying scriptures to reading *Total Money Makeover* by Dave Ramsey, we consumed it all.

We knew our goals seemed out there at the time, but we realized that we'd never be able to reach them if we didn't have a clear understanding of what they were. That plan became the living document that guided our lives. Although I didn't know it at the time, it shaped the thinking for me to develop the C-4 Approach to leadership and life.

REVISITING C-4

This whole book has been about an approach to *leadership,* and rightly so. If you picked it up and read what I've written, then you are a leader, regardless of title or position. Leaders influence. And the first person you've got to influence is you. Unless you get on track with your own mission and vision you'll make little progress.

As a reminder, here's what C-4 is all about:

➤ **CONSUME:** You must be a consumer of information, but what you consume is important. Learning to consume the right information, at the right time, is critical to your growth in any area of your life.

➤ **CONNECT:** Information is useless until you learn to connect the dots. This helps you use your insights to reach your goals and objectives in the fastest way possible while helping others do the same. Your life is connected because you are connected to your life.

➤ **COMMUNICATE:** The best leaders have an uncanny ability to stand up and articulate a clear message and get people galvanized around a common idea. They turn ideas into action.

➤ **COACH:** Leaders must reach up and down. Coaching others helps them connect their personal goals to the corporate goals so that both the person and the professional reach new heights.

I want you to use the C-4 Leadership Approach to shatter your glass ceiling and reach new heights in your professional career.

But I'd be lacking integrity if that's all I wanted you to do. That's because, like me, I know there is so much more to you.

YOUR FIVE LIFE DOMAINS

It's not a stretch to say that C-4 works in all areas of your life. If you recall from earlier, I made the point that C-4 Leadership was *intentional, focused, shaped,* and *stable*. Think about your life. Would you like those same adjectives to apply to all of it?

A life that's *intentional* is one that has a deep purpose and meaning. Intentionality is all about taking the right steps to a desired outcome and staying on track. It's investing in things that matter and ignoring those that don't. It's about creating a plan for your growth and development and sticking to it.

A life that's *focused* is free from distraction. It's not interested in keeping up with the Joneses because the Joneses don't matter. (No offense to the Joneses.) A focused life knows what's important and strives to reach those things. It's potent, powerful, and primed for action.

A life that's *shaped* is formed and functional. It has purpose and direction and meaning. It's built to the user's specifications rather than what the world tells it to be. It's flexible when necessary, yet rigid in the areas that matter.

A life that's *stable* is grounded, confident, and consistent. It resists the inevitable ups and downs of life and stays the course. It's led by the person that can be counted on to be quiet, calm, and assured regardless of circumstance or situation.

When I worked through the Plan 168 exercise, for the first time to see where my time was going, it opened my eyes to how *un*-intentional, *un*-focused, and *un*-stable I had been. It made me realize that I was never going to be able to *cash in* on my full potential until I'd discovered which areas of my life were worth focusing on and which needed to be overlooked or at least delayed.

I discovered there were five domains in my life that were critical to me: Faith, Family, Finances, Career, Community. I knew that if I could manage those well, then I'd design a life well-lived. I believe these domains will work for almost anyone, but I'd encourage you to create a list of your own domains that are important to you.

The C-4 Approach can be applied to any aspect of life once the goal is set. Here's how I applied the C-4 Approach to each of these areas:

➤ **FAITH** —It's taboo to talk about religion at work. I used to struggle with this because faith is the foundation of who I am. To effectively walk in God's purpose for my life, I simply connected the dots between faith and work by focusing on helping others reach their full potential.

➤ **FAMILY** —After three years of prayer, research, and procedures, we were able to have our daughter, Jordyn, and four years later, a son, Jaden. The pregnancies were not exactly flawless, to say the least, but the pain of the process is our constant reminder to appreciate the blessing.

➤ **FINANCES** —After consuming books such as Total Money Makeover by Dave Ramsey, podcasts, and YouTube videos, we paid off the bad debt and are now able to live as Ramsey would say "like no one else." Hint: It's not how much you make but where you sow it!

➤ **CAREER** —Coleshia and I are both at a stage now where purpose, passion, and profession have to line up. Amazingly, we've found that when you focus more on making a difference than making more money, your career takes off!

➤ **COMMUNITY** —My focus now is how to connect the dots between the poverty in my community and all that I've consumed in the area of STEM jobs. I've been sharing my C-student to C-suite story with inner city kids across the country so they can see it's possible. My new daily confession is to make an impact in my community that can never be erased! I can't wait to share those success stories with you.

WHERE CAN YOU BE BETTER?

In life, there is no standing still. You are either moving forward or backward. The truth is we can all be better in some areas of our lives. Life is a marathon not a sprint and you alone get to determine your destination.

Your thinking drives your behavior, and your behavior drives results. If you aren't getting the results you are looking for in any area of your life, it may be time for an explosion. The C-4 Approach is proven. It works. It's worked for me and many others.

Many people fail because they haven't decided where they want to succeed. I don't want that for you. I want you to take charge of your life, shatter the barriers that hold you back, and explode upward. *I believe you have what it takes within you.*

The question is, will you put it to work?

Only you can decide.

IN HIS TWENTY year career with FedEx, **Chris Winton** has moved from intern to IT Director to VP of Human Resources, but he still believes his best days are just ahead. In addition to his responsibilities at FedEx, he consults with top organizations like Google and The White House to help them develop innovative hiring solutions and empower their employees. His C-4 Leadership Approach equips people to break free from self-imposed limitations and create an intentional, life of significant success.

As a mentor, coach, and speaker, Chris has been featured on C-SPAN, recognized as one of the Top 40 under 40 in the *Memphis Business Journal*, worked with the Obama administration on Tech-Hire, received the 2018 HR Superstars Cream of the Crop Award from *HRO Today Magazine*. He's certified in culture shaping and human relations and is a successful real estate investor.

The titles he wears most proudly are Christian, husband, and father. Chris lives in his boyhood home of Memphis, TN with his wife Coleshia, daughter Jordyn, and son Jaden, where he's active in his community helping inner-city kids see that a bright future is possible with the C-4 Approach.

Connect with Chris to continue your growth journey and get free leadership insights and resources at ChrisWinton.com.

THERE ARE FAR too many people to list individually here who've had some positive influence on me and contributed to my growth and development as a person—and to this project in particular.

With that said, without the support and help of a few key people, I wouldn't be where I am today. And I certainly wouldn't have put this book together and carried it out into the world.

I want to thank my Father, James, for pushing me to always be better. Joel Olsteen once said your best friend is the person who brings the best out of you. Thank you dad for being my best friend.

I want to thank my Mom, Jenny, for ensuring Christ was always at the foundation of everything I did. Because of you, I understand what it truly means to be blessed and to be a blessing.

I want to thank my wife, Coleshia, for believing in me even when I didn't know who I really was. What I cherish most is our intimate conversations around dreaming big and the opportunities we can create for our kids and others in our community.

To my kids, Jordyn and Jaden, thank you for the constant reminder, the journey is the reward. Each day we laugh and joke together brings a joy to my heart far greater than the achievement of any career goal.

To Reggie Shaw, thank you for the open-door policy to your office and your home. You and Belinda welcomed Coleshia and I into your lives and gave us a fine example of how to successfully balance all of the domains within this thing we call life.

ENDNOTES

1 "Fred Smith," *Growth Strategies*, Entrepreneur, October 9, 2008, https://www.entrepreneur.com/article/197542.

2 Ron Shelton. *White Men Can't Jump.* Directed by Ron Shelton. 20th Century Fox, 1992.

3 M. Night Shyamalan. *The Sixth Sense.* Directed by M. Night Shyamalan. Walt Disney Studios Motion Pictures, 1999.

CPSIA information can be obtained
at www.ICGtesting.com
Printed in the USA
JSHW012319120320
4715JS00002B/2